The iPod Book

Doing cool stuff with the
iPod and the iTunes Store

Scott Kelby

FOURTH EDITION

The iPod Book, Fourth Edition

The iPod Book Team

TECHNICAL EDITORS
Cindy Snyder
Barbara Thompson
Jennifer Concepcion
Terry White

TRAFFIC DIRECTOR
Kim Gabriel

PRODUCTION MANAGER
Dave Damstra

COVER DESIGN AND
CREATIVE CONCEPTS
Felix Nelson
Jessica Maldonado

COVER PHOTOS
COURTESY OF
iStockphoto.com

PUBLISHED BY
Peachpit Press

Copyright © 2008 by Scott Kelby

FIRST PRINTING: November 2007

Composed in Myriad, Lucida Grande, and Helvetica by Kelby Publishing.

Trademarks
All terms mentioned in this book that are known to be trademarks or service marks have been appropriately capitalized. Peachpit Press cannot attest to the accuracy of this information. Use of a term in the book should not be regarded as affecting the validity of any trademark or service mark.

iPod, iTunes, Macintosh, and Mac are registered trademarks of Apple Computer. Windows is a registered trademark of Microsoft Corporation. Photoshop Elements is a registered trademark of Adobe Systems, Inc.

Warning and Disclaimer
This book is designed to provide information about iPods. Every effort has been made to make this book as complete and as accurate as possible, but no warranty of fitness is implied.

The information is provided on an as-is basis. The author and Peachpit Press shall have neither liability nor responsibility to any person or entity with respect to any loss or damages arising from the information contained in this book or from the use of the discs or programs that may accompany it.

ISBN-13: 978-0-321-52466-9
ISBN-10:   0-321-52466-7

9 8 7 6 5 4 3 2 1

Printed and bound in the United States of America

www.peachpit.com
www.kelbytraining.com

*For my best buddy
Dave Moser, for always
looking out for me.*

Acknowledgments

Although only one name appears on this book's spine, it takes a large, dedicated team of people to put a book like this together. Not only did I have the good fortune of working with such a great group of people, I now get the great pleasure of thanking them and acknowledging their hard work and dedication.

First, I'd like to thank my wonderful, amazing, hilarious, fun-filled, and loving wife, Kalebra. You're the best thing that's ever happened to me—you're part wonder woman, part supermom, part business exec, and part standup comic, and every day you manage to put a smile on my lips and a song in my heart. Your spirit, warmth, beauty, patience, and unconditional love continue to prove what everybody always says—I'm the luckiest guy in the world.

I also want to thank my 11-year-old son, Jordan. I'm so proud of him, so thrilled to be his dad, and I love watching him turn into the wonderful "little man" he has become. He has so many of his mother's special gifts, especially her boundless heart, and it's amazing the amount of joy he and his mom bring into my life.

Also, last year, the single best thing that can happen to a person happened to me— God blessed our family with the birth of an adorable, happy, healthy little baby girl— Kira Nicole Kelby. She's 21 months old now, and has the sweetest disposition a baby can have. I couldn't ask for anything more.

Thanks to my big brother Jeff for all the wonderful things you've done for me (and for other people) and for having so much of our dad in you. Your humor, generosity, and compassion are an inspiration. I love you, man.

Special thanks to one of my very best friends, Terry White. If there's anybody who knows more about the iPod and iTunes, I've yet to meet him, and that's why I had to have Terry tech edit this book. He did an amazing job (as expected), and his ideas, input, and suggestions made this a far better book than it would have been. I owe ya big time T-bone! (By the way, don't call him T-bone. He hates it. That's why I call him T-bone.)

A big thanks to my in-house tech editor Cindy Snyder, who worked with me on this latest edition of the book. She did just a wonderful job and was able to keep me on track, organized, and focused (and believe me, that's not an easy job).

Thanks so much to my "iPod Lifestyles" models: Brett Nyquist, Stephanie Cross, Jennifer Concepcion, Michael Cross, and Debbie Stephenson.

Thanks to my brilliant Creative Director Felix Nelson, for once again lending his creative ideas and input, which make every book we do that much better.

To my best buddy and book-publishing powerhouse Dave Moser (also known as "the guiding light, force of nature, miracle birth, etc."), for always insisting that we raise the bar and make everything we do better than anything we've done.

Much love to my amazing creative team at Kelby Media Group: You guys rock! (Plus, once again this year many of you have already shown great humility and class when losing to my Fantasy Football team, the "Oldsmar Thunder," and you should be commended. Now, everybody sing the Thunder fight song with me: "We hail thee Oldsmar Thunder. Our hearts are filled with pride. With voices strong...etc.")

I couldn't do any of this without the help and support of my wonderful assistant, Kathy Siler, without whom I'd be sitting in my office mumbling and staring at the ceiling. She's my right-hand-man (even though she's a woman) and makes my work life have order, calm, and sense. She is the best.

Thanks to my good friend Jean A. Kendra, for her support and enthusiasm for all my writing projects.

I owe a debt of gratitude to my friends at Peachpit Press, especially my publisher Nancy Ruenzel, and my editor Ted Waitt. They really "get it," and their philosophy and vision make writing books an awful lot of fun, which is very rare in this industry. Also, my thanks to Scott Cowlin for tirelessly finding an audience for my books.

Thanks to my mentors whose wisdom and whip-cracking have helped me immeasurably throughout my life, including John Graden, Jack Lee, Dave Gales, Judy Farmer, and Douglas Poole.

A personal thanks to my buddies Jeff Revell, Marvin Derezin, Rod Harlan, Mike Kubeisy, Dave Cross, Matt Kloskowski, Corey Barker, RC, Terry White, Larry Becker, and Felix, just for being my buddies.

Thanks to the whole team at Kelby Media Group, for their commitment to excellence, for refusing to accept limitations, and for being an example of what's best about this industry.

And most importantly, an extra special thanks to God and His son Jesus Christ for always hearing my prayers, for always being there when I need Him, and for blessing me with such a wonderful life, and such a warm, loving family to share it with.

About The Author

Scott Kelby

Scott is Editor-in-Chief and Publisher of *Photoshop User* magazine, and Editor-in-Chief and Publisher of *Layers* magazine. He is President and co-founder of the National Association of Photoshop Professionals (NAPP), the trade association for Adobe® Photoshop® users, and President of the software, education, and publishing firm Kelby Media Group.

Scott is a photographer, designer, and award-winning author of more than 45 books on technology and digital imaging, including the best-selling books: *The Digital Photography Book, The iPhone Book, Photoshop Down & Dirty Tricks,* and *The Photoshop Book for Digital Photographers*. Scott has authored several best-selling Macintosh books, including *Mac OS X Killer Tips, Getting Started with Your Mac and OS X,* and the award-winning *Macintosh: The Naked Truth*, from New Riders and Peachpit. He is also Series Editor for the *Killer Tips* book series from New Riders. His books have been translated into dozens of different languages, including Russian, Chinese, French, German, Spanish, Korean, Greek, Turkish, Japanese, Dutch, and Taiwanese, among others. Since 2004, Scott has been awarded the distinction of being the world's No. 1 best-selling author of all computer and technology books, across all categories.

Scott is Training Director for the Adobe Photoshop Seminar Tour, Conference Technical Chair for the Photoshop World Conference & Expo, and is a speaker at trade shows and events around the world. He is also featured in a series of Adobe Photoshop training DVDs, and has been training Adobe Photoshop users since 1993.

For more background on Scott, visit his daily blog, Adobe® Photoshop® Insider, at www.scottkelby.com.

Table of Contents

Chapter Four 69

It's Tricky

Cool iPod Tips & Tricks

Chapter Five 83

Cars

Using the iPod in Your Car

Table of Contents

Chapter Six 95

Video Killed the Radio Star
Video on Your iPod

Chapter Seven 119

Get the Freeze-Frame
Using Your iPod's Photo Features

Table of Contents

Table of Contents

Chapter Eleven   235

Imaginary Player

Playlists and Smart Playlists

Chapter Twelve   263

Tip Drill

Cool iTunes Tips

Table of Contents

Chapter Thirteen — 289

Add It On
iPod Accessories

Chapter Fourteen — 307

Lido Shuffle
How to Use Apple's iPod shuffle

Table of Contents

Chapter Fifteen   325

Cast of Angels

How to Download (and Create Your Own) Podcasts

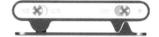

Appendix   343

Recommended Dose

**A Peek at My Own Personal, Ultra-Secret,
Yet Surprisingly Way-Cool Playlists**

Index   350

Don't Read This (just skip right to Chapter 2)

Chapter 2? Why not start at Chapter 1?
Because Chapter 1 is not for you. In fact, I wasn't even going to include a Chapter 1 at all (and simply start the book with Chapter 2), but I was afraid that somebody would buy the book and need Chapter 1 (not you, mind you, but someone).

Okay, so if Chapter 1 isn't for you, who's it for? Basically it's for freaks. See, here's the problem: When you first get your iPod, it's basically a brick. It can't do anything because it doesn't come with any songs or videos preloaded on it. Not a single one. Nada. So if you open the box and turn it on, it will have the same functionality as a brick—it will sit there in your hand doing nothing. Most folks (you, me, other non-freaks) understand that there are some things that need to be done before you use your iPod (you have to either download some songs, or import them from CDs, or import songs already on your computer, or download a podcast or TV show from the iTunes Store; then you have to organize your songs into playlists; transfer your song library into your iPod; learn a few things about how the iPod works; and then you have a fully functioning iPod that totally rocks). In short, you have to pay your iPod dues.

But there are people out there (you know who they are) who don't want to pay their dues. They only want one thing—instant gratification. They bought an iPod, and they want to use it now. They want to put the earbuds in, go immediately to the mall, and just "be seen" with an iPod. Oftentimes "these people" wouldn't even have a song on their iPod—they'd just fake it—bobbing their heads as if there were really music playing, but that's risky, because if they run into somebody they know, that person might say, "Hey, cool—an iPod. Can I hear it?" Then they're busted. So to get around that, all they would need to figure out is how to download (or import) just one song into their iPod as fast as possible, without learning anything else about the iPod or iTunes or the iTunes Store. Then they wouldn't have to pretend that they're hearing music; they would cover themselves from possibly enduring an embarrassing "moment of silence" with a friend. And they would become very well acquainted with that one song.

Well, that's what Chapter 1 is for—it shows those people ("them") how to do nothing more than quickly download one song and play it. So as long as you're not one of "them," you need to start at Chapter 2 and skip Chapter 1 altogether. Now, you probably know some Chapter 1 people, and when you lend them this book, tell them that they only have to read Chapter 1. They'll thank you for it.

Okay, I get the Chapter 1 thing, but didn't you say "Don't Read This" at the top of the page?
Right. That's because if instead it said "Introduction" at the top of the page (which is what this secretly is by the way), there's no chance you would read it. None. Nobody reads introductions these days. More people watch C-SPAN than read introductions (if that tells you anything). But the weird thing is, introductions are very, very important (after all, if you hadn't read this, you'd be needlessly reading Chapter 1 right now, right?).

Publishing companies have spent millions on researching the "nobody-reads-the-introduction" phenomenon, and the results of that research showed that so few people now read a book's introduction that publishers no longer edit or proofread introductions before they go to press. Want proof? Check this out: neeblick sanbo floppybobo. They have no idea what I'm writing here. "I cood litter dis ting wit typos unt dey wood never no." See what I mean? So basically, it's just you and me here, but if you continue reading this short introduction, I can promise you one thing: after you're done, you'll either say,

"Hey, I'm glad I read that" or "Now I fully understand why nobody reads introductions." Either way, you've come this far, so you might as well hang in there for a few more paragraphs. *[Hanging in there is hard to do.—Ed.]*

So, do I really start at Chapter 2?
Yes, really.

So what makes this book different from all the other iPod books out there?
There are basically two kinds of iPod books out there: (1) The "tell-me-all-about-it" kind, which tell you everything before you do anything. They include in-depth discussions on compression algorithms, debates about analog vs. digital equalizers, and they show things like how to export your playlist in Unicode format and how to dismantle and reassemble your iPod while blindfolded. (2) Then there's this book. It's not a "tell-me-all-about-it"; it's a "show-me-how-to-do-it" book. I show you how to do only the most important, most requested, most likely things you're going to want to do with your iPod so you can start using it now.

So how do I use it?
Each page in the book shows you how to do just one important thing. One topic. One idea. One feature. For example, if you want to have your iPod automatically balance the volume between songs, I will show you, step-by-step, how to do exactly that. No big discussions about recording techniques, room acoustics, or why some songs are recorded louder than others—just how to turn the sound balancing feature on. I skipped the information overload and all the tech-geek jargon, and I say everything the same way I would if you asked me to show you in person. So, when you want to learn a particular thing about your iPod, just find the topic in the Table of Contents, turn to that one page, and you'll have the answer you need in seconds. That's what makes it a "show-me-how-to-do-it" book. If at some point in the future you decide that you want to read in-depth discussions on compression algorithms, then you'll go buy one of those 500-page iPod books.

Is the book in some kind of order?
I'm glad you asked that. It's in some kind of order, just not the ideal one. In that I mean it's not in the real order of how you'd actually use an iPod from start to finish. In real life, the first thing you do is charge your iPod (which takes about four hours for a full charge), and while it's charging you'd go to work in iTunes (the software that lets you sort, arrange, and even buy music for your iPod), because that's what you really need to do before you really start using your iPod. So, really, the book should've been in this order: (1) two pages on charging your iPod, (2) a hundred or so pages on using iTunes and the iTunes Store, including how to transfer songs onto your iPod, and then lastly (3) how to use your iPod's features. That would be the ideal way to structure the book, but I didn't do it that way. Why? Because of human nature. When people buy a book on the iPod, they expect to open the book and see a lot about the iPod right off the bat. Seriously, think about it—if you went to the bookstore, picked up a book called *The iPod Book*, and instead of seeing a bunch of stuff about the new iPod you just bought, the first hundred or so pages is on some software you may not have even realized you need, you might put the book back down and keep looking until you found a book that's really about iPods.

Right? Well, I've put too much work into this book to take that chance, so I sold out (to "the man"), and put the iPod stuff right up front in nothing short of a slick, subliminal, mind-control marketing gimmick. I knew you'd understand. Hey, but by reading this introduction, you've now learned the real iPod workflow, giving you (come on, say it with me) "real value in reading this book's introduction." See, I told you this would pan out.

Okay, so if it's not in a workflow order, what kind of order is it in? I call it a "use-a-funkability" order. What that means is that when you get to the iTunes chapters, they're in order by what you'll probably wind up doing first, followed by what you'll do second, third, and so on. So even though the entire iTunes section is technically in the wrong place, the section itself is in the right order. So is the iPod stuff. So is everything else. So being in the right order in the little picture, while still not being in the right order in the big picture, makes this "use-a-funkability" work. Come on, say it with me out loud— "use-a-funk-a-bility." It's catchy.

Is this book for Windows or Mac users?
Both. The iPod and iTunes are identical on both Mac and Windows. However, in the iTunes chapters I give some keyboard shortcuts, and because the keyboard on a Mac and the keyboard on a PC are slightly different, I give the shortcuts for both.

What if I have an iPod touch or an iPod shuffle?
All the iTunes stuff still applies to you, but since these iPods have different controls from the iPod classic and iPod nano, I wanted to address them separately, so there is a separate chapter for the iPod shuffle (Chapter 14) and one for the iPod touch (and the iPod features of Apple's iPhone; Chapter 8). See, just when you think I'll zig—I zag. By the way, I have no idea what that means.

How did you know I wanted all these questions answered?
I've got a telekinetic thing going on. Actually, what I have is beyond that. It's called "tele-funkability." Gotcha! (I just wanted to see if you're still paying attention.)

What's with the chapter intros?
I start each chapter with a short intro. They're as meaningful in the complete understanding of the chapter's contents as the word "use-a-funkability" is to anything. In other words, they're for fun, too. I do that because the rest of the book is pretty straightforward stuff, and at some point, after writing page after page of "click here, scroll to that, insert that cable, etc.," I needed some space to break out a can of my inner funk-a-chunk-a-liciousness. I know, it's hard to believe I get paid for this.

Anything else I should know?
Nah—I think you're good. Though I do want to offer this closing thought: If after all this, you decide to go ahead and read Chapter 1, I won't tell anybody. Really, there's no shame in downloading one song and playing it over and over again in desperate hope of attracting some attention from the opposite sex (sorry about using the word "sex" in my book, but my publisher told me it will help sell more books). Okay, I think you're ready. Turn to whichever chapter you feel most drawn to. Either way, it won't be long before you've uncovered how to master Apple's iPod—the baddest portable music player the world has ever known. It's funk-a-fab-u-los-oh!

Chapter One

I Can't Help Myself

The Chapter for People Who Must Play a Song Right Now

Okay, just so you know—you're NOT supposed to read this chapter. This chapter is only for people who don't really care about learning how to use their iPod, how to use iTunes, or really enjoy the entire process of "ripping, mixing, and burning" (as Apple once called it). This chapter is for very shallow people who simply just want to play a song, just one song, right now. These people have the delayed gratification quotient of a gerbil, so they wouldn't care about "the right way" or "the best way"—they just want to play a song right now, no matter what. That's why I named this chapter after the Four Tops hit "I Can't Help Myself." Now, when you see that song mentioned, it's usually followed by "Sugar Pie, Honey Bunch" in parentheses, so you go, "Oh, that song," because there's been about 20 songs named "I Can't Help Myself." I went with the Four Tops version 'cause I'm about "a-hundred," and all the songs I know were written before you were born. But I don't care—you shouldn't be here. You should start at Chapter 2 (as I clearly stated in the book's introduction), and you darn well know it, so if you're here, you get what you get—old cliché song titles from a cranky old man. Now seriously, folks, I mean it—go to Chapter 2 and do this right. It's not too late to start putting your life together and that begins with making good decisions. For example, cut your hair. How are you going to get a decent job with that hair? And take down those hippie beads, and enough with the peace signs, and all that "flower power" stuff....

Read This Before You Read ANYTHING!

WARNING: Remember, read this first chapter only if you just bought your first iPod, and you're so excited about it that you just want to load a song and play it right this minute. Otherwise, skip to Chapter 2 and start there. Now, is what you would have learned in this short chapter the recommended procedure? Nope. Ideally you'd charge your iPod while working in iTunes (the free downloadable software that lets you organize and transfer music to your iPod). You'd import songs from CDs, download songs from the iTunes Store, and then create your own custom playlists (honestly, as you'll find out, this organizing and sorting stage is a lot of the fun of having an iPod). Then, once everything was organized in separate playlists and ready to go, during the three hours it takes to charge your iPod, you'd transfer the songs to it, and then you'd begin playing around with all the cool stuff on your iPod. But if you're reading this chapter, you can't wait three hours. You want to hear a song on your iPod right now (but there isn't one there yet; you have to put one there). Well, this chapter will show you how to download a song into your iPod so you can walk around listening to your *song*. Luckily, no one else will know you're listening to just *one* song, and you'll look approximately as cool as if you had actually done things "the right way." Will loading one song and listening to it now hurt anything? Nope. So why not do it? My point exactly—let's get to it.

Don't Charge Your iPod, Yet

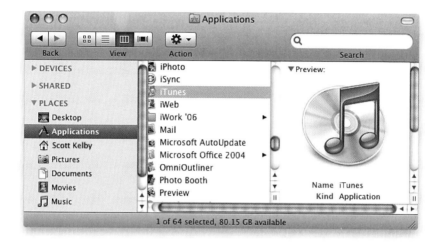

Because in this chapter we're doing the whole "play-one-song-right-now" thing, you can probably skip charging your iPod at this point, because iPods usually ship with enough battery charge to let you turn them on and play a few songs. The problem is: iPods don't ship with songs already on them (well, technically there was one iPod that did—the Special Edition U2 iPod from a few years back that came with a catalog of all of U2's songs already on it—but my guess is you don't have that iPod). Anyway, to get songs from your computer into your iPod, you use Apple's free iTunes software (for Mac or PC). If you've got a Mac, you're in luck because iTunes comes preinstalled on every Mac built in the past five or six years (just look in your Mac's Dock, and if the iTunes icon isn't there [it's a CD with musical notes on it], then you'll find it in your Mac's Applications folder). If for some reason you deleted it, you can download the latest version for free at Apple.com/itunes. If you have a PC, no worries, you can download iTunes free from the same place: Apple.com/itunes. So skip the charging for now, and instead launch iTunes (or if you don't have it yet, go download and install iTunes), and now you're ready to move on to picking your first song.

Picking Your Song

Okay, so you've installed iTunes—now what? Well, your song can come from three places: (1) you already have a song on your computer; (2) you can import a song from a music CD; or (3) you can buy a song from the iTunes music store (which we cover in detail later in the book). For now (just for now, where we're trying to play a single song as quickly as possible), we'll just cover options (1) and (2). We'll start with (1): If you have an MP3 song already on your computer's hard disk, then go under the iTunes File menu and choose Import, then navigate to where that MP3 is on your hard disk and click the Choose or Open button. The song will now import into iTunes, and you'll see it appear in your list of songs. Or should I say, your list of "song"? Easy enough. But what if you don't have a song on your computer? Well, that's covered on the next page.

What If There's No Song on Your Computer (Yet)?

If you don't have an MP3 song anywhere on your computer, then grab a music CD and put it into your computer's CD-ROM drive. The songs on your CD will appear within iTunes (they may appear as Track 1, Track 2, etc., but if you're connected to the Internet when you do this, it will probably pull the track names down for you automatically—more on this later in the book). A dialog will also appear asking if you would like to import the CD. For now, just click No. So, which song do you choose? If the track names got imported from the Internet, this is pretty easy—just choose a song you don't mind hearing over, and over, and over again. If the track names didn't get downloaded (and you see just Track 1, Track 2, and so on listed, then you can double-click directly on any track to hear that song. That way, you can hear each song, which will help you find the song you want to import. Now, you see all those little checkboxes that appear to the left of the song titles? Every song with that little box checked will be imported into iTunes, but you only want one song, right? So, press-and-hold the Command key (on a Mac) or the Ctrl key (on a PC), and click once directly on that little checkbox that appears to the left of your desired song's name. This "unchecks" all the songs (so nothing's getting imported). Now, click on the box in front of just that one song you want imported (as shown above), then click the Import CD button in the bottom-right corner of the iTunes window, and that song will be imported into iTunes. You're almost there.

Connecting Your iPod to Your Computer

At this point, you have a song imported into iTunes (either from your hard disk or from a music CD), and you're ready to copy that song you see in iTunes over onto your iPod. To do this, connect your iPod to your computer using the USB connector cable that came with your iPod (thankfully all iPods come with this connector). The smaller end plugs into any USB port on your computer, and the wider, flatter end connects to the bottom of your iPod. (*Note:* If your iPod came with an iPod Dock, which is a little stand that holds your iPod upright while it's connected to your computer, then the flat, wide end of the cable connects to the back of the Dock instead, as shown above). Just doing this—connecting this USB cable between your iPod and your computer—will launch iTunes (if it's not already open) and transfer the song to your iPod automatically (this process is called "syncing," because now iTunes and your iPod both have the same stuff. They're in sync). That's it—the song is on your iPod. It's almost time to jam.

---

iTip: If You Have a Firewire Cable

If you have an older iPod, it's likely that instead of a USB cable, your iPod came with a FireWire cable (also called an IEEE 1394 cable on the PC). It works the same way, you just plug the smaller end into your FireWire port (or IEEE 1394 port) instead of your USB port. Other than that, the syncing and everything else works the same.

Disconnecting from Your Computer

While the syncing process is under way, your iPod will say something along the lines of "Synchronizing: Do Not Disconnect," so…just sit tight until the syncing process is done. When the syncing process is complete, for just a few moments you'll first see "Ejecting: You May Now Disconnect" onscreen and then you'll see the iPod's main menu screen appear. Also, you can look at the status of the syncing process at the top center of the iTunes window. When the sync process is done, it will read, "iPod sync is complete," and your song will now be in your iPod. Once the syncing is complete, go ahead and eject your iPod from your computer by clicking on the little Eject icon that appears to the right of the iPod's name in the Devices list on the left side of the iTunes window (shown circled above).

Note: If you have an older iPod (like the original iPod nano, or an older iPod, etc.), it will display the main menu when the syncing process is done, too, but it also may instead display a large checkmark and the words "OK to Disconnect" on your iPod's LCD display. When either one of these messages appears on your iPod's display, you can unplug the cable from your iPod and your computer, because your song is "in there."

Connecting the Headphones

PHOTO BY SCOTT KELBY

To hear your song, you'll need to connect the headphones (called "earbuds"), which come included with your iPod. You plug these earbuds into the headphone input on the top of your iPod or the bottom of your iPod nano (as shown here). Just plug 'em in, then put the earbuds in your ears (I probably didn't have to include that whole "put 'em in your ears part," right?).

Waking Your iPod and Playing a Song

By the time you unplug your iPod from your computer, find your earbuds, and plug them in, it's quite possible that your iPod will have gone to sleep (to save battery life, which is important at this point since you really haven't yet charged the battery). To wake it, press the button in the center of your iPod (you can actually press any button, but since that one's the biggest, it makes an easier target). When you start, you'll be at the main menu, so to find your song, gently slide your finger in a clockwise rotation around the center wheel (called the Click Wheel) on the front of your iPod. You'll see the highlight bar move over the various items in your main menu as you glide your finger. Stop on Music (Music should have been highlighted when the main menu came up), press the center Select button, and when the Music menu appears, glide your finger along the Click Wheel until you have Songs highlighted, and press the Select button again. Now you'll see it—your song. Press the Select button in the center of the Click Wheel or the Play/Pause button below it, and glorious audio will pour through your earbuds like music playing through headphones (you didn't expect that metaphor, now did you?).

Pausing, Stopping, Hearing It Again

To stop your song from playing, press the Play/Pause button again. To continue the song, press that same button one more time (you play and stop using the same button. Okay, technically, you're not stopping the song, you're "pausing" the song, but you get the idea). Want to jump to the end of the song? Press-and-hold the Next/Fast-Forward button (the button on the right side). Want to hear the whole song again from the beginning? Press the Previous/Rewind button as the song ends. It's a vicious circle.

You Did It!

PHOTO BY SCOTT KELBY

That's it. You imported a song into iTunes, you copied that song over onto your iPod, and you played that song (probably multiple times) through your earbuds. Life is good. You've just literally scratched the surface of what the whole iPod experience is all about, and that's what the rest of this book is all about—showing you all the cool things you can do that make the iPod the amazing music player, video player, photo viewer, game player, cool thingy, etc., that has changed the music world forever. Now that you've gotten that "I've-just-got-to-play-a-song-now" thing out of your system, it's time to "do it up right." So turn the page and let's get to it.

Chapter Two
The Outsiders
How to Work the Stuff on the Outside of Your iPod

I'm not really thrilled about having the word "stuff" in the subtitle of this chapter, but since there really isn't an all-encompassing word that describes all the buttons, sliders, wheels, and inputs on the outside of your iPod, the word "stuff" works as well as any. Okay, what about the title "The Outsiders"? Well, that's a tribute to the 1960s band of the same name, who had a huge hit with the song "Time Won't Let Me," which has been licensed for use in numerous commercials. Considering that this chapter is about how to use all the "stuff" on the outside of your iPod, it's not all that bad a name. Now, how did I come up with that name? It's brilliant, really, but to understand how it came about (and to be there for the actual moment when it all came together), you'll have to read the introduction for Chapter 3. That's right, you have to read another chapter intro, even though by now you've probably realized that these chapter intros have less to do with what's in the actual chapter, and more to do with how late at night it is when I write these intros, and how many glasses of wine I had before writing them. Okay, the last line is made up to make me sound like a sophisticated writer who sips wine, smokes fine cigars, and types by the light of a roaring fire. It's a very romantic version of the truth, which is more like this: It's 9:14 on a Saturday night, I'm sitting at the kitchen table with a half-eaten delivery pizza from Westshore Pizza and an empty can of Caffeine-Free Diet Coke. See, I should've stuck with the wine story.

Where iTunes Fits In

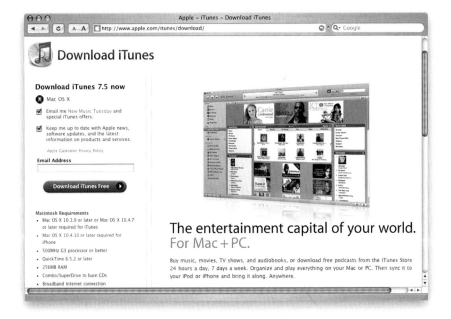

The software that copies your songs, movies, TV shows, podcasts, and photos from your computer to your iPod is Apple's iTunes (for Windows PCs and Macintosh computers). iTunes comes preinstalled on every Mac built since 2001 (if you can't find it, look in your Mac's Applications folder), and the Windows PC version is a free download from Apple.com/iTunes. But don't just think of iTunes as an "uploader" because it does so much more than that—it's your central entertainment hub, letting you organize and play all your music and videos right from your computer. In fact, a lot of the fun of this whole process is doing just that—organizing your music into playlists of your favorite bands, or favorite styles, or watching full-screen video on your home computer, or shopping for music and videos online at the iTunes Store (it's the world's most popular online music store). So, a decent chunk of this book is dedicated to teaching you the ins and outs of iTunes, because it's where you'll spend a lot of your time. iTunes has an awful lot of really dedicated (okay, fanatical) fans because it's some of the coolest, most fun software Apple's ever made, and although it's very easy to learn and use, it's surprisingly powerful. This is basically how the process works: you import music and video files into iTunes (or download them from the iTunes Store), and then when you connect your iPod to your computer, iTunes launches and whatever music and videos you have in iTunes gets copied automatically over to your iPod. It sounds pretty simple, and it is, so let's get started.

Importing Songs from a CD

Importing songs into iTunes directly from music CDs is easy: Just launch Apple's iTunes software, then put a music CD into your computer's CD-ROM drive. The songs on your music CD will appear listed within the iTunes main window (if this is a commercially produced CD, and you're connected to the Internet, iTunes will automatically add the song titles for you. If it's not a commercial CD—maybe this is mix CD you created, or a CD of a friend's band—your songs will appear with the generic names "Track 1,""Track 2," and so on). Either way, a dialog will appear asking, "Would you like to import the CD [name of CD] into your iTunes library?" If you click the Yes button, it copies all the songs on your CD onto your computer, and into iTunes. That's all there is to it. If you don't want all the songs imported, you can choose which ones to import by turning off the checkbox that appears to the left of each song (only songs with a checkmark get imported). By the way, if you only want one song imported, press-and-hold the Command (PC: Ctrl) key and click once on the checkbox beside the song you want. This unchecks all the other songs, but leaves that one checked.

---

iTip: Click the Import CD Button

If, for some reason, you don't get the little dialog asking if you want to import the songs from your CD into your iTunes Library, you can always click the Import CD button in the bottom-right corner of the iTunes window.

Importing Songs Already on Your Computer

If you already have songs on your computer, getting them imported into iTunes is a breeze. The fastest way is to just launch iTunes, and then literally drag-and-drop the songs from your computer right into the main iTunes window, and they'll be imported automatically. Another way is to go under the iTunes File menu (in the menu bar up top), and choose Import (or use the keyboard shortcut Command-Shift-O on a Mac, or Ctrl-Shift-O on a PC). This brings up a standard Import dialog, where you can navigate to the location of the song or video you want to import into iTunes. When you find the music or video file on your computer, click on it, then click the Choose or Open button and iTunes brings it on in. If you're connected to the Internet while you're doing this, iTunes will go and find the album art for the songs you've imported. It's that easy.

Downloading Songs from the iTunes Store

The iTunes Store is the groundbreaking, history-making online store that started it all, and it's so well designed that it really makes shopping for music, movies, TV shows, podcasts, games, and videos an awful lot of fun. To get to the iTunes Store, launch the iTunes software, then click on the iTunes Store link on the left side of the iTunes window (shown circled in red above). *Note:* This is an online store, so you have to have an Internet connection to access the store. There are so many cool features in the iTunes Store that I've got an entire chapter just on the iTunes Store (it's Chapter 10), but in short, here's how it works: You browse around the store looking for your favorite songs, movies, etc., and when you find one you want, you click the Buy button. You'll have to set up an account with the Store (it takes just a moment—and a credit card, of course), but then your download will begin and your song, movie, music video—whatever—will appear in iTunes. The next time you connect your iPod, whatever you bought at the iTunes Store gets copied over onto your iPod, but you have the option of listening to (or watching) your downloads on your iPod or on your computer right within iTunes itself (of course, if you have an iPod shuffle, which has no screen, you can only watch videos you download within iTunes. I guess you knew that, right?).

Creating a Playlist

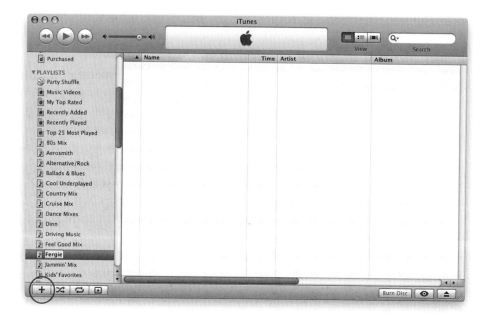

Once your music is imported into iTunes, it's just kind of in one big bucket—it's not sorted or categorized, it just appears in your Music Library in the order you imported it. That's why there are playlists. You make playlists to bring some sort of organization to your music collection. For example, you might want to create a playlist of just your favorite rock songs, or just '70s disco, or just alternative, or classical, or a playlist of just a particular artist (so you might have a playlist of just Fergie songs for when you're feeling Fergalicious), or you might create a playlist of sad songs, or slow songs, or a mix for a party you're throwing, or just romantic songs, or just your kid's favorite songs (you get the idea). Creating playlists is simple: You start by clicking the Create a Playlist button at the bottom-left corner of the iTunes window (it looks like a plus sign). This adds an empty playlist to your list of playlists on the left side of the iTunes window, and the name is already highlighted so you can type in a name for your new playlist, then press the Return (PC: Enter) key on your keyboard. To add songs to this new playlist, under Library (top left), click on Music, and then scroll through your collection. When you see a song you'd like in your playlist, drag-and-drop that song title right onto your new playlist in the Source list, and it's added to that playlist. Keep adding songs until you're done. Then, to play just the songs in that playlist, click on it, then double-click the first song, and the songs will play in order.

Customizing Your New Playlist

When you look at a playlist you've created, you'll notice that, by default, the songs in your playlist appear in the order that you dragged-and-dropped them into your playlist. Luckily, you can put your songs in any order you like by simply dragging them into the position you want. For example, if you want the fourth song to be the first song, just click-and-drag that song to the top of the playlist. As you drag a song up or down the list, you'll see a thin black line appear between tracks, showing you where your song will appear if you were to release the mouse button at that moment. When you do release the mouse button, the song moves to the position where the thin black line appears (this may sound a bit confusing, but if you try it once, you'll see what I mean). *Note:* If you double-click on a song in a playlist, it starts playing that playlist starting with that song. So, if you double-click on the first song, it plays all the songs in that playlist in order. If you double-click on the eighth song, it starts there instead and plays the rest of the songs in order until it reaches the end of the playlist (unless you have Repeat Playlist turned on).

Getting Music onto Your iPod

When you've got your songs arranged in iTunes just the way you want them (you've created playlists, put your songs in order, etc., like it shows in Chapter 11), it's time to get those songs onto your iPod. It sounds complicated, but it couldn't be easier. Using the USB 2 cable that came with your iPod, just connect the cable to your iPod, the other end to your computer, and it'll do the rest. The transfer is automatic—your computer will automatically launch iTunes and download your songs, playlists and all. (Watch the top of your iTunes window and when the transfer of songs is complete, you'll see the message, "iPod sync is complete.") If you have an iPod Dock, just sit the iPod in its Dock, connect the USB 2 cable to your computer, then sit back and relax.

Now you can click the little Eject button (within iTunes) to eject your iPod if you like, but it's not necessary (unless you're using your iPod as a hard disk). Okay, you're ready to take your show on the road (so to speak).

Turning Your iPod On and Off

As silly as this may seem (how to turn it on and off), I can't tell you how many people get tripped up by this because there isn't an "On/Off" button. So, how do you turn it on? Press any button on the front of your iPod, and it will spring to life (so in essence, every button is the "On" button). But it's not that way for turning the iPod off. To turn it off, press-and-hold the Play/Pause button for a couple of seconds and it will turn off. Some people get in the habit of turning the iPod on and off using the same button—they always press Play/Pause to turn it on, and they hold Play/Pause to turn it off. We call these people "sprenger" (which is the German word for "sprinkler"). I don't know why.

Navigating: iPods with a Click Wheel

All the iPods (except the iPod touch), are controlled using the round Click Wheel on the front of the iPod. There are five buttons on the wheel for iPods that have a screen—a Play/Pause button at the bottom, a Menu button at the top, a Previous/Rewind button on the left side, a Next/Fast-Forward button on the right side, and a Select button in the center. (*Note:* The iPod shuffle's wheel is different—see below.) You scroll up and down your iPod's menus by gliding your finger lightly around this wheel (like you're tracing a circle) in either a clockwise or counterclockwise motion. When you find something you want, you press the Select button in the center. Pretty easy stuff.

The iPod shuffle also has five buttons, but since there's no screen, they're slightly different: the center button is the Play/Pause button, and the left and right buttons rewind and fast forward like the standard iPods, but the top button (a plus sign) increases the volume and the bottom button (a minus sign) lowers the volume. There is no Menu button because there's no screen on an iPod shuffle. It adds to the mystery of it all (you can think of that last sentence as marketing copy).

Using the Click Wheel and Playing Songs

The Click Wheel itself is stationary—you're doing all the work by sliding your finger (or thumb) around the wheel, or pressing the buttons on the wheel.

The Click Wheel is really more like a touch pad with a built-in rocker switch (okay, that makes it sound more complicated than it is). Here's how it works: you touch it lightly with your thumb or finger and gently slide your finger around the wheel in either a clockwise or counterclockwise direction. So, if you're at the top of a menu and you want to move down the menu, press your finger lightly anywhere on the Click Wheel and start sliding your finger around it clockwise. To move in the other direction (up the menu), just slide your finger around the Click Wheel in the opposite direction. Once you get to a song you want to hear, you can either press the Play/Pause button at the bottom of the Click Wheel or just press the Select button in the center—either way, your song will play (hey, that rhymes).

---

iTip: Pausing a Song

If you're playing a song and you want to pause it, just press the Play/Pause button. Want to resume playing? Press the same button again. This button both pauses and plays, and that's why its icon has both the pause and play symbols.

Fast Forward in the Song

If you want to skip ahead in the current song, press-and-*hold* the Next/Fast-Forward button. The key word there is "hold" because if you just press the button once, the iPod will jump to the next song—you have to press-and-*hold* the button. Rewinding works the same way (but of course, press-and-hold the Previous/Rewind button instead).

Not Sure Which Song You Want?
Then Choose Music

If you're not sure exactly which song you want to hear, then you'll love the iPod's Music feature. Start at the main menu, and click on Music using the center Select button. Now you get to choose how you want to browse: by Playlists, by Artists, by Albums, by Songs, by Genres, etc. For example, if you choose Artists, you'll see a list of all the artists on your iPod (as shown above). See an artist or group you like? (Maybe Fergie or Janet Jackson?) Just click on their name, then click All Songs (if you have songs from multiple albums), and you'll see a list of all of their songs that reside on your iPod. It's kind of like a playlist of just their songs. Press the Play/Pause button and it's a Janet Jackson love fest. You can also browse by Genres (like all Jazz songs or all Alternative songs), which makes it easy to start playing the kind of music you're in the mood for, rather than having to pick songs one by one. Try browsing this way sometime. It rocks (an unintentional pun that should've been intentional).

How to Jump Back One Screen

If, at any time, you need to jump back to the previous screen, just press the Menu button at the top of the Click Wheel. Press-and-hold the Menu button and it takes you straight to the main menu.

Updating Your iPod with New Songs

If you've added new songs to iTunes (maybe you bought some songs from the iTunes Store or imported songs from a new CD), you're going to want to get these new songs onto your iPod. To do that, connect your iPod to your computer (using the Dock or the supplied USB 2 cable), and iTunes will launch and automatically update your iPod with the new songs. However, if your iPod was already connected to your computer when you bought a new song (or imported songs from a CD), you have to request an update by either: (a) going under iTunes' File menu and choosing Sync "Your iPod's Name," or (b) clicking on your iPod in the Source list on the left side of the iTunes window, then clicking the Sync button (as shown above).

Done Listening? Put It to Sleep

When you're done listening to your iPod for a while, you can put it to sleep two ways: (1) pause your music by pressing the Play/Pause button, and after a minute or two of being paused, your iPod will go to sleep to save battery life, or (2) hold down the Play/ Pause button for a few seconds and it will go to sleep (your screen will turn black). Your iPod remembers where you were in a song when it went to sleep, so when you wake it later, it picks right back up where you left off. Unless you leave your iPod asleep for 36 hours or more, in which case it falls into a Deep Sleep. You still wake it the same way (by pushing any button), but when you do, it's kind of cranky and wants coffee (sorry, I couldn't resist). Actually, after being in deep sleep, it starts up again from scratch (with the Apple splash screen and all), which takes longer than its normal nearly instantaneous waking because it has to go through a little startup routine.

How to Keep from Draining Your Battery

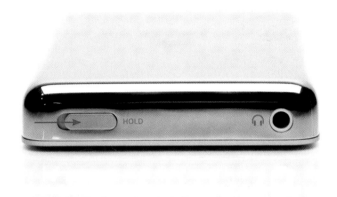

After you put your iPod to sleep, before you just go tossing it into your pocket, purse, backpack, computer bag, etc., I recommend sliding the Hold button (found on the top of the iPod) to the "on" position (so the orange part is visible). This locks the buttons on the Click Wheel, so something doesn't accidentally bump into it and turn your iPod on, needlessly draining the battery. If you're really low on battery life, try using the buttons as little as possible (they drain the battery, too), but the biggest battery-drainer of them all is the screen's backlit color screen, so if you're low on battery life, limit your time scrolling around through different menus, and you'll save battery life.

Turning On the Backlight

Backlight off   *Backlight ON*

What do you do if you're in a dark, smoky London club on Playlist Night, but it's too dark in there to see your playlists (after all, it's not just dark—it's dark and smoky)? Here's what to do: just press anywhere on the Click Wheel and your iPod's Backlight will come on, illuminating your screen like a beacon in the night.

Battery Saver: Controlling Your Backlight Time

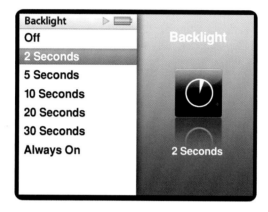

If you really want to stretch your iPod's battery life between charges, this is the first place to stop. If you can get away with turning the Backlight timer feature off altogether, other "Podders" will envy your longevity. If you can't go "Backlight free," try setting it so it just comes on for two seconds (as shown here), and you'll conserve quite a lot of battery power. You find this control by going to the main menu, scrolling down to Settings, and pressing the center Select button. When the list of settings comes up, click on Backlight. This brings up a screen with choices for how long your backlight will stay on—from two seconds (probably too short to be practical) to Always On (ideal for people who don't roam more than a few feet from their battery charger). Just find the setting that seems right for you and click on it to set your new Backlight timer.

Controlling Your Screen's Brightness

The ability to change the brightness of your screen serves a major purpose—extending your battery life. That glorious full-color screen draws a lot of battery power, and if you don't need the screen at its full brightness (for example, you're on a flight at night and the cabin lights are dimmed), you can lower the brightness by quite a bit, and extend your battery life. To control the brightness, go to the main menu and choose Settings. Then scroll down to Brightness and press the Select button. There you'll find the Brightness slider. The default brightness is 50%, so it ships from the factory at about half of its maximum brightness. You adjust the brightness level the same way you do volume—you scroll the Click Wheel to the right to make it brighter or to the left to make it less bright (and save even more battery life).

Charging Your Battery (Using the USB Cable)

When you get an iPod, the first thing you need to do is charge the battery. Luckily, each iPod includes a USB 2 cable that lets you charge it by plugging it into your computer. Here's how: Take the cable and insert the thin flat side into the slot at the bottom of your iPod. Then connect the other end of the cable to the USB port on your computer. That's it—your iPod is charging and you'll either see a big battery charging indicator icon or the Connected…Eject Before Disconnecting screen in the iPod's LCD display. If you need to disconnect, first eject your iPod by clicking on the little Eject icon that appears to the right of your iPod's name in the Devices list. Then you can safely unplug your iPod without damaging any music or video files on your iPod.

Charging Your Battery (Using the Dock)

Perhaps the most convenient way to charge your iPod is to use an Apple Dock—you just sit your iPod in the Dock (as shown above), and it syncs your iPod and charges it. There are three advantages to the Dock: (1) it's easier—because you don't have to connect the USB cable to the bottom of your iPod each time; (2) it puts your iPod upright (so you can see the screen, rather than just having it lying flat); and (3) you can use an Apple wireless remote to control your iPod while it's in the Dock. Once you have your Dock, you just plug the flat end of the included USB 2 cable into the Dock (that's the end you would normally plug into the iPod itself), then plug the other end into the USB 2 port on your computer, and you're set! (Note: If you have an iPod nano, it comes with a special white plastic adapter that drops into the standard dock slot so it will hold your nano upright, too.)

How's Your Battery Life?

Is it time to charge your battery? Just take a quick peek in the upper right-hand corner of the iPod's screen and you'll see a little battery indicator. If it's solid, you're in good shape. If it's half-full, then you're an optimist. (Get it? Half-full? Ah, forget it.) Actually it means it's got half of a full charge. If the battery indicator is clear, it means it's time to recharge your iPod battery by plugging it into your computer, or putting your iPod in the Apple Dock (provided you have one, of course).

---

iTip: Battery Charge Is "Use It or Lose It"

There's a weird thing about iPods. If you don't use them for a time, the battery charge slowly drains. For example, if you've fully charged your iPod for a trip that's coming up in four or five days, chances are when you get on the plane, plug in your head-phones, and sit back to enjoy your air jams, the battery will be dead. This is a classic case of "use it or lose it." The drain is likely caused by the iPod's internal clock that ticks even while the iPod is off. Also, there's no power to USB ports while a computer is sleeping, so if your computer goes to sleep with your iPod connected, your iPod will stop charging and go to sleep, too.

Replacing Your iPod's Battery

Eventually your iPod's battery will reach the point of no return (it won't hold a charge any longer), and you'll have to get the battery replaced. Well, I have good news and bad news. The good news: even with lots of use, your iPod's battery will last for quite a while. The bad news: this isn't one of those "drive-down-to-Wal-Mart-and-buy-a-new-battery-for-$4.99" situations. iPod batteries aren't cheap (as of the printing of this book, Apple charges $59, plus shipping, for a new iPod replacement battery), and they should be replaced by a qualified technician (like a tech at the Apple Store in the mall). If you can't spring for the full $59 battery from Apple and the technician's fee for replacing it, you've got a few options. One is to go to PDASmart.com. They'll provide and install a new iPod battery for you for $45 to $55 (plus shipping), depending on the generation. Not bad. There's also iPodResQ.com, where for around $54, they'll give you a new iPod battery, do the install, and ship your iPod back to you within 24 hours (the shipping's included). Considering the cost, this is why it's a good idea to get AppleCare for your new iPod for around $59 ($39 for the nano or shuffle), which would cover a battery replacement if you needed one.

Using External Speakers

Although iPods were born to be used with headphones, today there are a lot of speaker systems custom designed for iPods. In my opinion, the three hottest external speaker systems are the Bose SoundDock Digital Music System, $300; the Klipsch iGroove HG speakers, $200; and Apple's iPod Hi-Fi system, $349 (you can buy these at the Apple.com Store). All three have a built-in cradle (it's like a Dock) that your iPod sits in while playing, and all automatically charge your iPod at the same time. Only one bad thing—although all work with regular iPods or the iPod nano, only Apple's iPod Hi-Fi officially supports the iPod photo. However, I've read that the Bose SoundDock comes with different-sized Dock adapters, and that the largest one does accommodate the iPod photo, but I haven't tested it myself, so....

Playing Video on Your iPod

If you have one of the newer iPods, iPod nanos, or an iPod touch, you can play TV shows, movies, and music videos, which you can buy and download from the iTunes Store. Then, when you sync your iPod with iTunes on your computer, any videos you've purchased from the Store will be downloaded onto your iPod. To play these videos, go to the main menu and click on Videos. In the Videos menu (shown above), scroll down to the type of video you want to play and click the center Select button. For example, if you click on TV Shows, any TV shows you've downloaded will be listed here. To play a particular show, scroll down to it, then press the center Select button to see a list of episodes. When you find the episode you're looking for, press the center Select button again (or just press the Play/Pause button).

---

iTip: Create Video Playlists

Just like playlists for music, you can create playlists for videos, as well, with collections of your favorite TV shows, movies, or music videos. For example, you could create a video playlist of Black Eyed Peas videos, or videos of dance music, or classic rock videos, or… well, you get the idea.

Chapter Three
Pod's Theme
iPod Essentials

I originally had the idea that I would name the previous chapter "The Outside" because it would cover everything you do on the outside of your iPod (like charging the iPod, connecting it to your computer, and using all of the buttons that appear on the outside of your iPod. Makes sense, right?). Then, I would follow up by calling this chapter "The Inside," because we'd touch on all the stuff that appears onscreen—so basically the stuff that controls the inside of your iPod. It seemed like a brilliant plan, until I realized that the idea absolutely stinks. That's because when people looked through the book's Table of Contents, what would chapter subtitles like "Inside" and "Outside" mean to them? Nothing. Couple that with a chapter title like "The Outsiders" (for the 1960s band), and then it would look like this: "Chapter 2: The Outsiders: Outside." See, it just stinks. Now, if it said "The Outsiders," and then it said, "How to Work the Stuff on the Outside of Your iPod," that certainly would help. Okay, could you please just close your eyes for a moment while I talk to my editor? (Dear Editor: Is it too late to change the previous chapter's name to "The Outsiders"? It's not? Great!) Okay, now open your eyes. Hey, good news! We're going to go with "The Outsiders" for that chapter name after all. But for this chapter, on what happens on the inside—I'm stuck. How about "Pod's Theme" by Lesion? Easy enough—let's go with that (am I saying this stuff out loud?).

Customizing the Main Menu

The iPod has a main menu that is kind of the starting place for making your way around the different areas of your iPod. You'll wind up using this main menu a lot, and that's why you'll want to customize it so the features you use most are right there at the top level (reducing your need to dig down through different menus). Here's how to customize yours: Start at the main menu and, using the Click Wheel, scroll down to Settings. Press the center Select button, then scroll down to Main Menu and press Select again to see a list of menu items. You can choose which ones you want to appear in your main menu by toggling them on or off using the center Select button (items with a checkmark beside them will appear in the main menu).

---

iTip: Getting to the Main Menu

With the iPod, everything pretty much starts at the main menu, and since you'll find your-self going back there fairly often, you might as well learn how to get there at any time—just press the Menu button three or four times and you'll be back at the main menu.

Searching for Songs Made Easy

The iPod has a Search feature to help find just the song (or artist) you're looking for fast. Hold down the Menu button to jump to the main menu; click on Music, then scroll down and click on Search. When the Search menu appears, you'll see the alphabet near the bottom of the window. Scroll to the first letter of the song, or album name, or artist's name, then click the center Select button and it instantly starts searching and gives you results live as you enter each subsequent letter. For example, if you're looking for Nickelback, as soon as you select N, it instantly (and I mean instantly) lists every song, or album, or artist on your iPod that begins with N. When you move over to I and press the Select button, now it's every song, or album, or artist that begins with "Ni." By the time you press C, you've narrowed your search down pretty well (on my iPod, it lists Nickelback, and then "Have a Nice Day" by Bon Jovi, because "Nice" contains "Nic"). If you choose a wrong letter, you can use the Previous/Rewind button to delete it, and if you need to put a space between words, press the Next/Fast-Forward button. When you're done searching, press the Menu button, and the search bar goes away, and your search results appear in the window. Now you can just click on the song, or album, or artist you want. The whole process is much faster than it sounds. Try it once, and you'll use it again and again, as there's really no faster way to get right to the song you want.

Visual Searching with Cover Flow

If you're a visual person, you might prefer to search for songs using Cover Flow, which displays the album cover art of the songs on your iPod (as shown above). That way you flip through covers and when you see the album cover for the song you want, you just click the center Select button and it displays the songs from that album! Start at the main menu, select Music, and then click on Cover Flow. Now you can scroll through your entire library by sliding your finger around the Click Wheel, and just stop when you see the album you want. It's probably not as fast as searching by name, but it's way more fun.

Using Your iPod as a Stopwatch

Your iPod comes with a stopwatch feature, complete with a lap timer. This is great for timing your workouts, or if you're a runner, or…there's probably another good reason to have it on there, but danged if I can think of one. Did I mention it's good for timing workouts? Wait, wait…how about timing eggs (to music)? Anyway, here's how it works: Hold down the Menu button to jump to the main menu, then scroll down and click on Extras. Now scroll down to Stopwatch and click on it. To start the stopwatch, just press the center Select button. To stop it, press the Play/Pause button and a screen of options will appear (shown above), where you can choose to restart the timer, clear the log of laps (each time you start and stop the stopwatch, the iPod automatically logs it—to see the full list in detail, with stats, click on Current Log), or create an entirely new timer. One thing I think is particularly cool is that although it gives you a digital readout of the time, the analog stopwatch graphic moves in real time. It serves no other real function than being cool to look at, but hey—what's wrong with that?

Rating Your Favorites

Even though you probably have a lot of songs on your iPod, they're not all "your favorite song." Obviously, you like some better than others, and choosing which ones you like best (rating them from one to five stars) can be very helpful in making sure you hear your favorites more often. That's because once you've rated your songs, you can sort them so that your favorites (five stars) play first, then your next favorites (four stars), and so on. (Better yet, you can create a Smart Playlist where iTunes automatically compiles just your four- and five-star songs—more on that in Chapter 11!) You can rate your songs in iTunes, or right from your iPod while they're playing. Just press the center Select button twice and the stars-rating window will appear. Scroll the Click Wheel clockwise to add stars, and counterclockwise to take them away.

---

iTip: Updating Your Ratings

If you're rating your songs, it doesn't matter where you rate them—whether it's within iTunes or right on your iPod—because when you next update your iPod, any new ratings (no matter where they came from) are synced between the iPod and iTunes. Your ratings will then be updated in both places automatically, so they're always up-to-date. Cool, ain't it?

How to "Scrub" through the Current Song

Apple borrowed the concept of "scrubbing" from the world of digital video editing, and what it lets you do is quickly jump ahead (or back) to any point in the song while the song is playing. To scrub (while a song is playing), press the Select button once then slide your finger clockwise around the Click Wheel to scrub forward, counterclockwise to scrub backward. A progress bar appears onscreen to give you a visual cue as to where you are in the song (closer to the end, closer to the beginning, in the middle, etc.). When you remove your finger from the Click Wheel—the song starts playing from that point.

Getting to Your Playlists

To hear the songs in any one of your playlists, press the Menu button a few times until the main menu appears, use the Click Wheel to scroll to Music, then press the center Select button. Now choose Playlists to see a list of all your playlists. When you find the playlist you want, press the center Select button (but you're not done yet). This displays all the songs in the playlist you selected, but which song do you want to start with? Scroll down to the song you want to hear and press the center Select button again (or the Play/Pause button—either one will do it). Your song will begin playing, and when it's done, the next song in that playlist will play, and so on.

Shuffling Your Song Order

Once you choose a playlist and start playing a song, the songs will play in the same order you had them when they were in iTunes (so if you had them sorted by name, songs that start with the letter "a" would play first, then songs that start with "b" and so on, etc.). After a while, you'll hear a song and you'll already know what the next song is going to be. That's why you might want to turn on the iPod's Shuffle feature, which plays your songs in a totally random order (you can either shuffle all the songs in your Music library, or just songs in your current playlist). To shuffle all the songs in your entire library, hold down the Menu button to jump to the main menu, then scroll down and click on Shuffle Songs to turn this feature on. If you're in a playlist, playing a song, and you decide you want to shuffle that playlist, press the center Select button three times in a row and a shuffle control bar will appear at the bottom of the song window (as seen above). You can use the Click Wheel to choose Songs (which shuffles by song title), Albums (to shuffle by album), or Off.

Repeating the Current Song or Playlist

If you're really hung up on a song (like "Girlfriend" from Avril Lavigne, which must be heard hundreds of times in succession to really appreciate it), hold down the Menu button to jump to the main menu, scroll down and click on Settings. Now scroll down and click on Repeat to repeat only the current song (the little graphic on the right side of the screen will say "Repeat Current Song"). Press the center button again to repeat the current playlist (the graphic will say "Repeat Current Playlist"), and a third time to turn the Repeat feature off (the graphic then reads, "Play Current Playlist Once," which is a complex way of saying "Off").

Importing Songs Already on Your Computer

If you already have songs on your computer, but they're not yet in iTunes, here's how to import them: Launch iTunes, then go under the File menu and choose Import. When the Import dialog opens, navigate your way to the folder of songs on your hard disk, then select the songs you want to import and click the Choose or Open button to import those songs into iTunes. Easy stuff.

---

iTip: Getting Your Own Videos on Your iPod

Besides videos, movies, and TV shows you download from the iTunes Store, you can also get your own videos onto your iPod. You start by downloading the video onto your computer. Then, open your video clip in QuickTime 7 Pro (if you don't have it, it's available at Apple.com for both a Windows PC and a Mac). Once it's open in QuickTime 7 Pro, go under the File menu and choose Export. In the Export dialog, for your export method choose Movie to iPod from the pop-up menu, then hit the Save button and the converted movie file will appear on your computer. Drag it into iTunes, then connect your iPod and sync up. That's it!

Which Song Formats Work with Your iPod?

If you're wondering how you can actually fit thousands of songs on something as small as an iPod, it all comes down to this—compression. The songs you download onto your iPod are either in MP3 format (which is a music compression technique that makes the file size of your songs fairly small, while maintaining nearly CD quality) or AAC format, which is the format used by the iTunes store that features higher-quality sound and very small file sizes. (*Note:* There are two AAC formats: the protected AAC M4P, which is encrypted to prevent music piracy; and the unprotected AAC M4A, which is typical of imported audio CD files.)

Finding Out How Much Space Is Left for More Songs and Videos

If you're wondering how many more songs or videos you can fit on your iPod, here's a quick way to find out: From the main menu, scroll down and click on Settings. Then, on the Settings menu, click on About to see a horizontal bar graph of your iPod's available memory. If you want to see exactly how many songs and videos are on your iPod, then click the Select button again. To help you in your calculations, you can figure an MP3 song takes up about 4 MB of space (an AAC-encoded song, like ones downloaded from the iTunes Store, takes up a little less). Adding 125 songs takes up only around half of 1 GB, so if you see your Free amount is 12 GB, you can load a few thousand more songs and still have plenty of room. Video, however, eats up loads of space, with a typical music video gobbling up 25 MB. Believe it or not, that's really not bad, because a TV show eats up around 450 MB, and a full-length movie can take up anywhere from 750 MB to over 2 GB. So, if you're a movie freak, I hope you bought an 80-GB or larger model.

iTip: Using iTunes to Check Free Space

Another way to know how much room is left on your iPod for adding more songs and videos is to check in iTunes. When your iPod is connected, just click on your iPod's icon in the Source list on the left side of the iTunes window. Then look down along the bottom center of the main window and you'll see a readout that shows how much space is used, and how much space is still free for adding more songs or videos.

Deleting a Song from Your iPod

If a song you really hate winds up sneaking its way onto your iPod (this sometimes happens to a song you liked at one time, but after a few dozen plays, it really starts to get on your nerves), you can delete it from your iPod. The easiest way is to just delete the song from your playlist in iTunes, then plug in your iPod to your computer. When the iPod syncs, the offending song is gone!

Creating a Playlist Right within Your iPod (On-The-Go)

Although we normally create playlists on the computer within iTunes, you do have the ability to create one custom playlist from right within your iPod. It's called an "On-The-Go" playlist and to add a song to your On-The-Go playlist, just press-and-hold the center Select button until the song title (shown above) blinks three times (it only takes a few moments). That's it—it's added to your On-The-Go playlist (you can also add an entire album, or even the contents of a playlist, the same way). When you've added enough songs to your On-The-Go playlist, you can get to it at the bottom of the Playlists menu. When you click on the On-The-Go playlist, at the top you'll see a listing for Save Playlist. Click on this if you decide that you want to turn this On-The-Go playlist into a regular playlist. This clears your On-The-Go Playlist, so you can create a new fresh one whenever you're in the mood. If you just want to clear the list and start over, choose Clear Playlist.

---

iTip: Syncing the On-The-Go Playlist

When you sync your iPod with your computer, your new On-The-Go playlist will appear in iTunes, and you can add songs, delete songs, and reorder them just like you would any other playlist. When you're done, in iTunes first click on your iPod (in the Devices list on the left side), then click the Sync button to send your changes to the On-The-Go playlist over to your iPod.

Making an On-The-Go Song Go Away

Have you ever added a song to your On-The-Go playlist and thought, "Ya know, I'm not sure I want that song on there?" For example, if accidentally, in a moment of confusion and uncertainty, you somehow added a Spice Girls song to your On-The-Go playlist (I'll tell ya what I want [what I really, really want]. I want that song off my playlist). Luckily, deleting that song from your On-The-Go playlist is as easy as accidentally adding it was. Just find that song in your On-The-Go playlist and click-and-hold the Select button until the song flashes three times. That's your cue that the Spice Girls are gone.

---

iTip: Adding an Album to Your On-The-Go Playlist

Here's a little-known tip: you can add more than one song at a time to your On-The-Go playlist. In fact, you can add an entire album, or all the songs from a particular artist— just find the artist (or album) on your iPod, then press-and-hold the center Select button until it flashes three times, and all those songs are added.

Controlling Your iPod's Volume

To turn your iPod up, glide your finger lightly clockwise around the Click Wheel, and to lower the volume (yeah, right), rotate your finger around the Wheel counterclockwise. The moment you start sliding either way, a Volume Bar will appear so you can see how loud (or soft) your volume setting is, and this bar grows longer/shorter as you increase/decrease the volume.

Enhancing Your Sound Quality (EQ)

You're about to uncover a feature of your iPod that can make your music sound so much better, you'll never turn this feature off again (and sadly, it's off by default). Your iPod has a built-in sound equalizer that can change the audio output of your iPod so it sounds best for the type of music you listen to—and best of all, all you have to do is choose from a list of built-in presets. Here's how it works: Hold down the Menu button to jump to the main menu, use the Click Wheel to scroll down to Settings, and press the center Select button. Scroll down to EQ and press the Select button again. You'll see a list of preset EQs for various musical genres (e.g., R&B, Hip Hop, Jazz, Spoken Word, Acoustic, Classical, etc., plus special EQ settings that boost the bass, boost the vocals, or reduce the treble). Just scroll down to the type of music you listen to, click the Select button, then go back and listen to your music again. You will be absolutely amazed at how much richer, fuller, and just flat-out better your music will sound.

Saving Your Ears from Volume Abuse

Has this ever happened to you—you're walking down the street listening to your iPod, and a song comes on that's so loud you have to rip the earbuds out of your ears just to keep from blacking out? Thought so. That's because the recorded volume of songs can vary greatly from song to song. Luckily, there's a feature called Sound Check that can come to your rescue. Sound Check automatically balances the volume between songs so you don't suddenly get your ears blasted right off your head. However, this ear-saving feature is turned off by default—you have to go turn it on. Here's how: Hold down the Menu button to jump to the main menu, scroll down and click on Settings, then scroll down to Sound Check. It's turned off by default (the graphic on the right side of the screen will read "Use Original Volume Level"). So click the center Select button once to turn it on, and the graphic on the right side will now read "Normalize Volume Across All Songs, " which will bring peace and balance to your life (ah, if it were only that easy).

Using Your iPod as a Watch

Besides playing music, being your individual PDA, and perhaps even running slide shows, your iPod can also function as a clock—and it can even display the current time while you're playing songs. To see the current date and time, start by holding down the Menu button, which takes you to the main menu. Then click on Extras, and scroll to Clocks (it's at the top of the list of extras). This displays an analog clock with the current time, and it displays the date below the clock (as shown above). Once you've set your time (under Settings, under Date & Time), you can have your iPod display the current time while you're playing a song. To do that, start at the main menu and click on Settings. Scroll down and click on Date & Time, and when the Date & Time list of options appears, click on Time in Title to turn this feature On. Now the current time will appear up in the left-hand side of your Title Bar when playing a song.

---

iTip: Monitoring Multiple Time Zones

If you need to monitor time zones for different parts of the world (you international jet-setter, you), your iPod has the ability to view up to four different clocks—one for each different time zone. You set it up by going to the main menu and clicking on Extras. In the Extras menu, click on Clocks, then press the center Select button again. Choose Add or Edit, then choose your time zone by Region, and then by City, making you look and feel very intercontinental.

Setting an Alarm

Want to make sure you get to traffic court on time? Use your iPod's alarm function. Start at the main menu, scroll down to Extras, then click on Alarms. In the Alarms menu, click on Create Alarm (as shown here) and now your iPod's alarm will sound—you just don't know when. Luckily, there's a list of alarm options where you can choose the date and time you want this alarm to go off, whether you want it to repeat (to go off every day at that same time, which is ideal for habitual flaunters of traffic law), and you even get to choose the sound your iPod will wake you with (either an audible beep or a playlist of songs, but if you choose the playlist option, you'll need to connect your iPod to an external set of speakers, so you can actually hear your wake-up playlist. Of course, you could sleep with your headphones on, but I don't recommend it—they could come off while you're sleeping and before you know it, you're in contempt of court). You can also assign a label to your alarm to help you see at a glance which alarm you've set is for what, and you can also delete an existing alarm here, as well. Okay, your alarm is set. At the time you specified, your iPod will "alarm you."

---

iTip: Syncing Your Date & Time

Did you notice that your iPod seems to already know today's date and current time? That's because when you sync your iPod to your computer, it automatically sets your iPod's date and time. If you want to change it, go to Settings and choose Date & Time.

Turning Off the Click Sound

While you're scrolling around through the menus, your iPod makes an audible "click" sound. This is basically audio feedback so you know "things are happening" as you're scrolling around. This clicking sound drives some people mad (you know who you are), and they want it turned off. Plus, there are instances in which you don't want anyone to hear those clicks, lest they realize that you're playing with your iPod when you should be watching the console at the nuclear power plant. So, if you'd prefer "the silence of the Pod," you can stop the scrolling click sound by starting at the main menu, then scrolling down to Settings, and clicking on Clicker to turn the scrolling sound off. Press the center Select button again to turn it back on.

Playing Your iPod's Built-In Games

Okay, while it's not exactly a PlayStation 3, your iPod does come with some decent little games already installed. To get to these little gems, start at the main menu, scroll down to Extras, and then press the Select button. In the Extras menu, scroll down to Games and press the Select button to reveal the built-in games. These include iQuiz, Klondike (Solitaire), and Vortex. Press the center Select button to choose a game—and watch the hours just fly by. Of course, you can buy much better games from the iTunes Store (including classic arcade games like Pac-Man); see the next page for the full scoop.

Downloading Real Games

As I mentioned on the previous page, iPods come with some built-in games, and for lack of a better term, we'll say they're "cute" (there is a better term, I'm just not going to say it). But thankfully, Apple has introduced some pretty cool "real" downloadable iPod video games (some were commissioned by Apple, and some are existing games retooled for the iPod), available from the iTunes Store for $4.99 each. To buy these games, go the iTunes Store and click on the iPod Games link in the list of Store links on the upper-left side of the Store window. A couple of important things to note: You can't play these games within iTunes—they only play on your iPod, and once you download one (or more), they get copied over to your iPod the next time you sync. Once a game is on your iPod, you can play it by going to the main menu, then going under Extras, looking under Games, and you'll find it there (you use the Click Wheel as your game controller).

---

iTip: Using Downloaded Games

When you buy an iPod game from the iTunes Store, a new section appears in your iTunes Source list: iPod Games. You can see the games you own there, and clicking on a game title gives you the full game instructions (which is actually pretty handy), but remember—you can't play the game in iTunes, only on your iPod.

Listening to Audiobooks on Your iPod

The next time you're taking a trip, you might want to consider taking along a few audiobooks. Not only is the iPod designed to play audiobooks, but the iTunes Store also sells them. (The iPod also supports audiobooks downloaded from Audible.com.) To buy an audiobook, go to the iTunes Store, then click the Audiobooks link on the left side. If you find a title you like and download it, when you sync your iPod you'll find your audiobook by starting at the main menu, choosing Music, and pressing the center Select button. Then scroll all the way down to the bottom, where you'll find Audiobooks. Also, in case you were wondering, when you stop listening to an audiobook, your iPod notes the spot where you stopped, so when you go back to it at a later date, it picks up right where you left off (kind of like a digital bookmark). Better yet, this feature also works in iTunes—even when you sync it with your iPod, they update each other, keeping track of where you left off.

---

iTip: Changing Narration Speed

With audiobooks, you'll learn that sometimes the narrator's pace is just right, sometimes it's too slow, and sometimes it's too fast. Luckily, you can change that. Just press the center Select button four times until the word "Speed" appears in the lower-left corner. To the right, you'll see the word "Normal" (which, thankfully, is the default speed of audiobooks). To speed things up, just scroll the Wheel to the right and it changes to "Faster." If you want it slower, scroll to the left until the speed setting reads "Slower."

Renaming Your iPod

If you want to give your iPod a new name, first connect your iPod to your computer. Let's say, for example, that you want to change the name of your iPod to "Scott Kelby's iPod." (Hey, don't laugh. That's what I named mine and I really like it.) Then double-click directly on its name in the Devices list (on the left of the iTunes window) and its name field will highlight, ready for you to type in a new name (it's spelled "S-c-o-t-t"). Press the Return (PC: Enter) key on your keyboard to make the renaming complete.

Keeping Your iPod's Software Up-to-Date

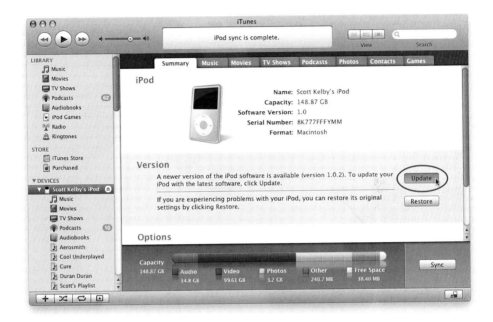

Apple updates the iPod software on a very regular basis, adding enhancements, little tweaks, etc., so it's good to make sure your iPod stays up-to-date. This is especially true if you have a number of different iPods. To see if your iPod software is up-to-date, and to install the latest iPod software if it isn't, just connect your iPod to your computer, then in iTunes click on your iPod in the Source list on the left side of the iTunes window. This brings up the iPod Preferences in the main window. From the Summary page, you can tell if your iPod software isn't up-to-date (as seen in the Summary page above). You can click the Update button (as shown) and it will update your iPod with the latest version of the software.

Chapter Four
It's Tricky
Cool iPod
Tips & Tricks

Using a Run-D.M.C. song as the name of a chapter on iPod tips and tricks gets me some props. Some street cred, because no matter how young and cool some of my readers might be, they can't dis Run-D.M.C. because they helped put rap on the map, and rappers of all ages still give them respect. (Notice how I used the terms "props," "street cred," and "dis" in the opening? I did that as a shout-out to my homies and peeps. See, there I go again, using that hip street talk all the kids are using these days.) Look, here's the deal: When you're a middle-aged white guy, all you remember are the slang terms used when you were growing up. Then you start listening to stations like Mix 100.7 and Oldies 104, and you never hear new street slang again. So the old street slang still sounds "new" to you. So, when you're in a situation where you're desperate to sound cool again (as I clearly am here), you instantly revert to words you remember were once cool. Like "props" and "dis." You might even throw in an occasional "chillin'," or if you're really old, you might actually call someone a "jive turkey" (believe it or not, there was a time when people under the age of 18 would use that term [with a straight face], and other people would think they were cool). So now I just sit around listening to old Salt-N-Pepa songs and repeating every cliché ever uttered on early editions of *Yo! MTV Raps*. Well, gotta go—my posse's hookin' up with another suck'a crew. (Forgive me.)

Getting Important Info about Your iPod

If you want all the background info about what's going on inside your iPod, the best place to get that is from within iTunes itself. Just connect your iPod to your computer, and then in iTunes click on your iPod in the Devices list on the left side of the iTunes window. This brings up the iPod Preferences window with loads of info about your iPod. In fact, there's so much info, it has to be separated into different tabs that appear across the top of the window. The first section that appears is the Summary tab, which shows the basic info for your iPod (your iPod's serial number, the total capacity of your iPod, etc.), and below that is a section where you can update your iPod software, or restore the original factory settings if you need to erase everything and completely start from scratch. Below that is a set of options for your currently connected iPod, and at the bottom is a graph that shows how much of your iPod storage space is used up, and the color bars show what they're taken up with. The tabs across the top of the Preferences window vary depending on which iPod you have connected, but you can think of them as preference settings for your particular iPod. For example, to set your preferences for which playlists are downloaded into your iPod, click on the Music tab. To decide which podcasts are downloaded into your iPod, click on the Podcasts tab. Do you see where this is going? Good, because one more "To decide which…" and I was going to have an aneurysm.

Using Your iPod as a Removable Hard Disk

That title is kind of misleading, because your iPod actually *is* a hard disk, so it's not like you're fooling it into believing it's a hard disk—it already knows it. However, for it to *act* like a regular hard disk (where you can store regular data, text files, Photoshop files, videos, etc.), you have to tell it that it's okay to do this. Start by connecting your iPod to your computer, and the Preferences Summary tab automatically appears. On the Summary tab, in the Options section, turn on the checkbox for Enable Disk Use. (*Note:* You only need to turn this option on when you have the "auto-update" feature active in the iTunes Preferences. Otherwise, if you've chosen to update your iPod manually, the Enable Disk Use feature is on by default. See the next page for clarification.) Your iPod will now appear on your desktop, and you can add files by dragging-and-dropping them onto the iPod icon, just like any other removable hard disk. This is great for moving non-music files between machines. There's one thing to remember though: when it's in this "disk" mode, you have to eject your iPod manually by Control-clicking (PC: Right-clicking) on the iPod icon (either on your desktop or in the iTunes Source list) and choosing Eject in the contextual menu that appears.

Turning Off iPod Auto-Updating

Each time you connect your iPod to your computer, iTunes automatically starts an updating (auto-synchronizing) process that transfers onto your iPod any new songs you've downloaded in iTunes, so your iPod is always up-to-date. It also deletes from the iPod any songs you may have removed from your iTunes Music Library, to keep iTunes and your iPod always "in sync." So, if you're not downloading new songs often, or you're not ready to take certain songs off the iPod, or your iTunes Music Library is larger than the amount of space on your iPod, you might not want it automatically syncing every time you put your iPod in its Dock just for charging—especially since this syncing ties up your iPod and iTunes. If you'd prefer to update your iPod manually, you can turn off this "auto-syncing." Here's how: While your iPod is connected to your computer, click on your iPod's icon under Devices on the left side of the iTunes window. When your iPod's Summary tab appears, choose Manually Manage Music and Videos (or choose Manually Manage Music if you don't have a video iPod). Now you're in charge of syncing, and here's how it works: Look to the immediate left of your iPod in the iTunes Source list and you'll see a gray triangle. Click on it to see all the playlists on your iPod. To update your iPod manually, just drag a song from your iTunes Music Library (at the top of the Source list on the left) and drop it where you want it on one of the iPod's playlists. If it sounds like an awfully manual way to sync, that's because it is.

Troubleshooting: Your iPod Won't Turn On

If your iPod won't turn on, most likely it's one of two things: (1) Check to see if your button lock (that Hold button on top of the iPod) is turned on. If it is, all buttons are locked. Slide it over so you don't see the orange indicator any longer (which unlocks all the buttons), then press any button to turn on your iPod. If that doesn't do the trick, then go to Plan B: (2) It's probably the battery. Try plugging your iPod into your computer using the USB 2 cable. If neither of these two solutions works, try resetting your iPod (using the instructions on the next page).

What to Do If Your iPod Locks Up

If your iPod locks up (meaning, it's on, but you can't get it to do anything—you're stuck on a screen and the buttons don't do anything, the Click Wheel doesn't click, etc.), you can reset your iPod, which will usually do the trick (don't worry—resetting won't erase your songs or playlists). To reset your iPod, just slide the Hold button (that button on top of your iPod or bottom of your nano) over to the lock position (so the bright orange color shows), and then slide it back again to unlock it. Now hold down both the Menu button and the center Select button until the Apple logo appears in the LCD window (this usually takes less than 10 seconds), then release both buttons. If you have an older iPod, you still slide the Hold button to the lock position and then unlock it, but you press-and-hold the Play/Pause button and the Menu button instead. If you're not sure how old your model is, also try sliding the Hold button, then press-and-hold the Play/Pause button and the center Select button. One of those three combinations is bound to reset an older iPod.

Your iPod as Contact Manager

You can make your iPod act like a mini-PDA by having it store your contacts (addresses, phone numbers, etc.). If you're on a Mac and you're using Apple's Address Book application (which comes with every Mac), it couldn't be easier—just connect your iPod to your Mac (which launches iTunes). Click the Contacts tab in the iPod Preferences window. In the Contacts tab, turn on the Sync Address Book Contacts checkbox. You can choose to synchronize all of your contacts, or selected groups only. If you have not upgraded to at least iTunes version 4.8, you will have to open iSync from your Applications folder instead. (It's easier to just update your iTunes, so go ahead and do that first.) If you're using a Windows PC, when you turn on the Sync Contacts From checkbox, you will have to choose which program to synchronize with (Windows Address Book, Outlook, etc.) from the adjacent pop-up menu. If you haven't updated your iTunes, it's a little more involved, but it's still easy. Once your iPod is connected, open your contact manager and then drag addresses (your vCards) directly from your contact manager into the Contacts folder on your iPod. (*Note:* To access the iPod's Contacts folder, you'll first have to set the iPod to act like a hard drive, which we covered earlier in this chapter.) Once you've loaded your contacts, you'll access them the same way as mentioned above for Macs.

Putting Playlists in the Order You Want Them

Playlists appear in your iPod in alphabetical order (which makes sense). But what if you want a particular playlist at the top of the list (maybe your favorite playlist)? You can do that pretty easily by pulling an alphabet scam—basically, you just add an asterisk (*) before the playlist's name. For example, if your favorite playlist is called "Dance Mix," you'll just double-click directly on the playlist's name (in the Source list on the left of the iTunes window) and rename it with an asterisk before the playlist's name (so it would now be named "*Dance Mix." Now that playlist will appear at the top position (but it still won't move above any Smart Playlists). Easy enough, eh?

---

iTip: What to Do If Your Earbuds Disconnect

Wanna know a way-cool secret that Brett Nyquist (NAPP Web Developer and iPod addict) was kind enough to share? If you're jogging, walking, or getting into a fistfight, and you happen to yank out the earbuds from your iPod, the song that's currently playing will pause. All you have to do is plug the earbuds back into the headphone jack, press the Play button, and continue throwing punches. Your song will pick up right where you left off.

A Playlist Just on Your iPod but Not in iTunes

If there's a playlist that you want to appear just on your iPod (maybe it's a playlist you use when jogging, and you never play it in iTunes while sitting at your desk eating a Snickers), you can have this playlist appear *only* on your iPod. Just connect your iPod to your computer, then turn on the manual update feature (covered earlier in this chapter). Now click on your iPod in the Source list on the left side of the iTunes window and click on the gray triangle to its left to show a list of the playlists already on the iPod. Now click on the Create a Playlist button in the bottom left-hand corner of the iTunes window, and a new empty playlist will appear within the list, with the name field already highlighted (so type in a name, then hit the Return [PC: Enter] key on your keyboard to lock it in). Now drag-and-drop songs directly into this "iPod Only!" playlist, knowing that this playlist will appear *only* on your iPod and won't be adding useless clutter to your regular list of playlists (being the neat freak that you are).

Making Smarter Smart Playlists Using Keywords

Back a couple of years ago, Apple added the ability to embed your own keywords into an MP3 and, because they're embedded, when you move a song from one computer to another, these embedded keywords go right along with the songs. Now, how would you use this? Let's say you're a DJ at a party next week. As you go through your songs, you find ones you might want to use at the party, so you can go under the File menu and choose to Get Info on each song. Then, click on the Info tab at the top of the resulting dialog, and in the Grouping field enter your keyword, "Party," and click OK. Then, when it's time to put together a mix for the party, you can have iTunes create a Smart Playlist by choosing New Smart Playlist from the File menu, and in the resulting dialog, choose Grouping from the first pop-up menu; in the second menu choose Contains; and in the text field enter "Party." When you click OK, all the songs with the keyword (Grouping) of Party (regardless of their genre) will appear in your new "Party" Smart Playlist. It makes the Smart Playlist feature even smarter.

Making Sure All Your Songs Are Rated

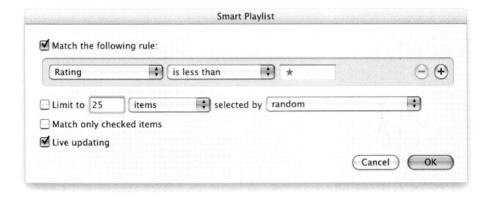

By now you can see how important it is to rate your songs (especially if you want to make Smart Playlists, and believe me—you want to make Smart Playlists). But you know (and I know) there are songs you haven't rated yet. Well, here's a quick way to find all your unrated songs and gather them in one place so you can rate them. Press-and-hold the Option (PC: Alt) key and click on the Create a Playlist button in the bottom-left corner of the iTunes window to bring up the Smart Playlist dialog. From the first pop-up menu choose Rating; from the second menu choose Is Less Than; in the stars field click on the first dot to assign the ranking of one star; and then make sure the Limit To checkbox is turned off, so it will get all your unrated songs. Click OK, and iTunes will instantly assemble a playlist of nothing but your unranked songs. Start playing a song from that list, and as soon as you rank the song—boom—it jumps off the Smart Playlist. When you're done, connect your iPod, and iTunes will add your new rankings there as well. See, that wasn't as hard as you thought it would be.

Safeguarding Your iPod with Screen Lock

Screen Lock enables you to lock your iPod's screen (using password protection), so if it were to fall into the hands of some scurrilous ne'er-do-well (a thief, or worse—your little brother), the screen would be locked, rendering it pretty much useless. To turn this feature on, start at the main menu, then go under the Extras menu, where you'll find Screen Lock. Select Screen Lock, and first you'll want to set your combination (numeric password). Selecting Screen Lock brings up a screen where you use the Click Wheel to choose the numbers you want as your passcode (you press the Select button to confirm your first number, and it automatically highlights the next number field over, but you can also move from field to field using the Previous/Rewind and Next/Fast-Forward buttons). Once you finish entering all four digits of your passcode, you'll be asked to confirm those numbers (yup—you have to enter all four digits again), and if you confirm all four numbers correctly, a little bar appears where you get to choose whether to Lock your iPod or Reset the passcode (which turns the locking off). If you choose Lock, it shows a large lock icon onscreen. To unlock your screen, press the center Select button and enter your passcode.

---

iTip: If You Forget Your Passcode

If you forget your passcode, all is not lost—just reconnect your iPod to your computer, and when it resyncs it automatically unlocks your iPod, because after all—it knows it's you. By the way, if someone enters the wrong passcode, they'll get an Incorrect Combination message, and the lock icon will reappear.

Chapter Five

Cars
Using the iPod in Your Car

So you're thinking, "Oh, The Cars—I love that band," but the title of this chapter isn't "The Cars," it's just "Cars," named after the punk rock song "Cars" by Gary Numan. Okay, you're now probably thinking, "The name Gary Numan sounds familiar, but not the song 'Cars.'" That's because the name of the song really should have been "In Cars" (ahh, now you recognize it). Even if you were born after 1980, if I sing a few lines, you'll probably recognize it (from when your parents listened to oldies stations). Here we go (ahem): "Here in my car, I feel safest of all. I can lock all my doors. It's the only way to live, in cars" (Da dunt…da dunt, da dunt). See, I told ya. Now, if I had written that song, I would've used entirely different words. For example, instead of "Here in my car," I would've written "Well shake it up baby now," and when he wrote "I feel safest of all," I would have written "Twist and shout." Am I crazy, or do my words just sound "right"? I dunno, maybe it's just me. And how about his second line? I mean, come on! Where he wrote "I can lock all my doors," I would've written "Every breath you take," and where he wrote "It's the only way to live," I would've written "Every move you make." This lyric stuff is easy. Anyway, this chapter is about using your iPod in your car, and all the different ways you can make that happen. What's nice is, once it's connected, you can ride around like I do, coming up with amazing lyrics. Seriously, they just pop in your head. Like for instance, just yesterday I came up with "Here she come now, sayin' Mony Mony!"

Full iPod Integration for Luxury Cars

When I wrote the first edition of this book, you basically had to own a luxury car (BMW, Mercedes, Ferrari, Infiniti, Volvo, or Acura) to have your iPod fully integrated into your car's audio system using Apple's "officially sanctioned" connection system. But things have changed since then and now we're "sticking it to the man" by having full iPod integration in a wide range of cars (including most GM, Ford, Chrysler, Dodge, Volkswagen, Nissan, Honda, Mazda, Jeep, Mini, Audi, and Scion vehicles, among others). In fact, Apple has an entire webpage dedicated to the auto manufacturers who offer full iPod integration (shown above). This integration lets you connect your iPod directly and control your iPod just like you would your built-in CD player or radio, and you can change songs, see which song/artist is playing, change playlists—you name it. Plus, if your car has controls on the steering wheel for your audio system, you can now control your iPod the same way, and let me tell you—that's pretty darn sweet. Now, of course, there are some limitations as to which models are supported and in what configurations. That's why the rest of this chapter exists—because full integration isn't available for every car yet. Well, that and the fact that sometimes the integration unit and installation labor charges from your dealer will add up to far more than your iPod cost you in the first place. Of course, if you own a BMW, or Mercedes, or Ferrari, or any one of those "bling-bling mobiles," the installation charges might not be a big concern. Visit www.apple.com/ipod/carintegration for direct links to these manufacturers' websites.

If Your Car Doesn't Offer Integration, Try This

If your car doesn't appear on Apple's full integration webpage, all is not lost. That's because many cars today offer the next best thing—a built-in auxiliary plug that lets you plug your iPod into your audio system and listen to your iPod through your car's speakers. However, it doesn't give you full control of the iPod, you still have to change songs, playlists, etc., on the iPod itself, but you'll have control over your iPod's volume, because you can raise and lower the main volume of your car's stereo your iPod is play-ing through. But hey, at least you're hearing your iPod through your car stereo and that ain't bad, and all you had to buy was the simple little cable (see the next page) that lets you go from the headphone jack on your iPod to the auxiliary input in your car (there's a better solution coming up on the page after that if you don't mind spending a few more bucks than just buying a cable). Now, how do you find out if your car has this little auxiliary input plug? Just go to the car manufacturer's website and type "iPod" in their search field. That's how I found the page you see above, on Lexus' website, that shows that the 2008 Lexus IS series comes standard with an auxiliary input plug for MP3 players (like iPods).

Here's Where to Find That Cable You Need

If you can't get full iPod integration, but you're lucky enough to have a car that has an auxiliary input plug, you're about 30 seconds from iPod integration—you just need a connector cable. You could go the inexpensive route and buy a 3.5mm male-to-male audio cable from Radio Shack—plug one end into your iPod's headphone jack and the other end into the stereo's auxiliary plug, and crank up the volume. Easy and cheap. The problem is your iPod's battery will keep running down, and you'll have to either buy a separate car charger or keep taking your iPod out of the car to charge it between drives (which is a total pain—believe me, I've done it). So, instead, I recommend the Belkin Auto Kit for iPod with Dock Connector. This simple kit does it all—it connects to your auxiliary plug (using the dock connector on the bottom of your iPod) and it charges your iPod at the same time, so your iPod's battery doesn't run down. It comes with a volume amplifier so you can adjust the volume of your iPod separately. (I know I recommend a few Belkin products throughout the book, but don't worry, they don't give me any compensation of any kind. Every Belkin product I have, I bought.) The downside to this charger? It's a bit pricey at around $40. You can find it at Belkin.com.

Kensington FM Transmitter for iPod

One way to hear your iPod through your car's stereo is to use a wireless FM transmitter, which lets you literally beam the music from your iPod to an FM station on your car's radio. Perhaps the most popular iPod FM transmitter today is the Kensington Digital FM Transmitter/Auto Charger for iPod, which not only broadcasts your iPod's music to any open FM channel on your car stereo, as the name implies, it also charges your iPod during the process. The unit attaches to your iPod's Dock connector, then plugs into your car's cigarette lighter (or auxiliary power input), and beams the signal to your FM stereo. Apple sells the Kensington FM Transmitter at the online Apple Store, at the Apple Store in your local mall, or you can get it directly from Kensington at Kensington.com.

---

iTip: It Comes in Colors

The Kensington FM Transmitter comes in either black or white to match your particular iPod. Well, as long as you don't have a blue or green iPod nano. Or a red one.

DLO TransDock Deluxe All-in-One Solution

If you have a luxury car, you need the first-class solution—the DLO TransDock Deluxe, which puts four popular accessories into one single unit: (1) it broadcasts your iPod's music through an open channel on your FM car stereo, (2) it charges your iPod using your car's built-in charger, (3) it acts as an iPod mount, supporting your iPod in an upright position so you don't need an iPod cup holder or other support to put your iPod within easy reach, and (4) it gives you a wireless remote control that connects to your steering wheel, giving you the closest thing to car-manufacturer quality integration. Plus, it comes with an A/V cable that lets you play your iPod's video content over your car's DVD screen (provided, of course, that your car has a DVD player and screen). It comes with two interchangeable faceplates (one silver, one black) for matching the look of the unit to your car's interior. The DLO TransDock Deluxe is available from Apple's online store, the Apple Store in the mall, or from DLO themselves at DLO.com for around 130 bucks.

iPod Holder for Your Car—You Need One More Than You Think

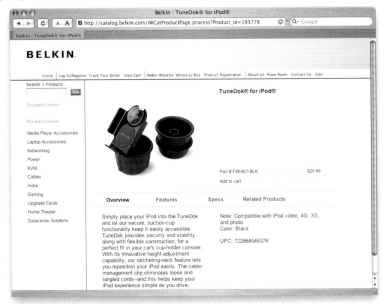

There are a few iPod-in-your-car options that come with an iPod holder, but most don't; and once you connect your iPod to your car, you're likely to find that the iPod doesn't have a secure home (in other words, it's just sliding around in the car, falling off the console, sitting in an unused ashtray, etc.). Luckily, you have a couple of decent options, my favorite being Belkin's TuneDok for iPod, which fits in one of your cup holders and, with its snug-fitting pocket, acts as a convenient home for your iPod. The only real downside is that you lose the use of one of your car's cup holders. It sells for around 30 bucks. You can buy these at Belkin.com.

XtremeMac Airplay Boost FM Transmitter

Want yet another choice for wireless FM transmission? Then how 'bout the XtremeMac Airplay Boost? This one's available from Apple's website, the Apple Store in the mall, or direct from XtremeMac.com. Unlike some wireless transmitters, it also charges your iPod at the same time, so not only are you not draining your iPod's battery, you're charging it. Best of all—it's inexpensive at only $49.95.

Control Your iPod without Losing Control

And then there is the high-tech solution (from Harman Kardon) that adds a high-tech looking screen to your dashboard, and a controller near your gear shift, which lets you change songs, playlists, and generally control your iPod without taking your eyes off the road. It's called the Harman Kardon Drive + Play, and the screen gives you a similar look and feel to the iPod's own built-in screen, but since it's larger (and mounted on your dash), you can just glance over and make changes instead of reaching for your iPod while you're driving. A lot of people who can't get full integration from their car manufacturer really like this solution, which despite its high-tech look, costs only $79.95, and you can find it at the Apple.com Store, or find a local retailer at Harman-Kardon.com

Third–Party Car Integration Kits

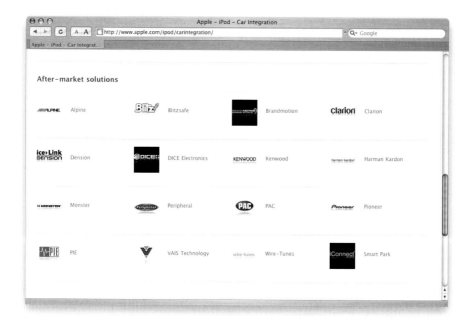

If you go to Apple's webpage showing the companies that support factory-made iPod integration (www.apple.com/ipod/carintegration), and you scroll all the way to the bottom of that page, you'll find a listing of all the companies that now provide third-party solutions (no factory or Apple-made solutions) for getting your iPod integrated into your sound system, where you have control over your iPod without having to touch the iPod itself (so it is integration—just not from the factory). The Alpine kits are very popular, as are the Clarion (which comes with its own motorized 7" LCD screen) and Harman Kardon kits (I mentioned Harman Kardon's solution earlier).

Wireless Control for Your iPod

If you're plugging your iPod into an auxillary MP3 jack in your car, you get to take things up a notch by going wireless, using Monster's iEZClick Remote Control for iPod. What's particularly nice is that it's RF-controlled, so your iPod can be out-of-sight and still be controlled by the wireless controller (while many wireless units have to have the iPod in its "line-of-sight"). It's lightweight, with large easy-to-use buttons, and it only costs between $50 and $70 at the Apple online store or from MonsterCable.com.

Chapter Six
Video Killed the Radio Star
Video on Your iPod

Okay, I admit the title for this chapter, a chapter on using video (TV shows, movies, and music videos) on your iPod, is just too obvious. But this song, lame as it was (is), has an important place in pop music history, for it was in fact this song that was the first video ever played on MTV. That's right, when MTV first aired, they aired the music video for the Buggles' "Video Killed the Radio Star." Now, if you've never heard this song, it's worth downloading from the iTunes Store and listening to (once) in iTunes. However, I don't recommend listening to it while driving (if you have your iPod connected to your car audio system), because it will subconsciously make you want to drive your car straight into the nearest stationary object. But, besides being a catchy-sounding name for this chapter, how does this song title relate to what's in this chapter? Well, it actually relates to a real-life story. I was producing a radio podcast (along with my cohorts, Dave Cross and Matt Kloskowski) called "Photoshop Radio" and each week we would share Photoshop tips along with some of the lamest attempts at humor ever recorded digitally. However, when video podcasting came along, and Apple made iPods with video playback capabilities, we killed the radio show and started *Photoshop®User TV*. So, in effect, video killed our radio podcast. Now, I know what you want to ask, "Okay, that makes sense, but how does your real-life story relate to this chapter?" Actually, I was hoping you wouldn't ask that.

95

Where to Find Videos for Your iPod

The iTunes Store sells three different kinds of video—full-length movies, TV shows, and music videos (plus there are a number of network TV shows you can download from the iTunes store absolutely free). Buying video from the iTunes store is covered in the next few pages, but you can also download free video podcasts, which are video programs created by everyone from individuals, to independent production companies, to big networks like ESPN and HBO. Lastly, you can import your own videos (home movies, free videos you download from the Web, etc.) into iTunes and then copy those onto your iPod. To import one of these types of videos, just drag the video clip into the iTunes main window and it will import automatically. If for some strange reason that doesn't work, then just go under the iTunes File menu and choose Import. On the next page, we'll look at downloading videos from the iTunes Store.

Music Videos from the iTunes Store

We'll start with music videos. To view the current selection (new music videos are added frequently), click on the iTunes Store link under Store on the left side of the iTunes window. Under iTunes STORE (on the top-left side of the main iTunes Store page), click on Music Videos. This takes you to the main page for music videos. In the center is cover art for the most popular music videos right now, and you can scroll through the selections using the scrubber bar below the covers. If you see a cover for a video you're interested in, just click on it to go to that video's page (in the example shown above, I clicked on Alicia Keys' cover to jump to the page for her music video of the hit song "No One"). Once on a video's page, you can either: (a) watch a 30-second preview clip of the video by clicking on either the round Preview button or on the cover art (shown in the window above), or (b) buy the video, which then downloads into your iTunes, and then onto your iPod when you sync it to your computer. And that's how you get videos onto your iPod— you buy them (they're $1.99 each) from the iTunes Store, they download onto your computer, then when you plug in your iPod, it updates your iPod with your newly purchased videos. If you decide you want to go back and search for a different video instead, click the Back button at the top-left corner of the main window.

Downloading Individual TV Shows

TV shows are available from the iTunes Store, as well, and you get to them pretty much the same way—you start by clicking on the iTunes Store link on the left side of the iTunes window, but then you click on the TV Shows link on the top-left side of the iTunes Store homepage. Like the music videos, it takes you to a main TV shows page, where you can choose from different genres (listed on the left side of the window). You can also view shows by network, view the list of top-downloaded shows, or just scroll down the page to see all sorts of different lists. With TV shows, you can buy an individual episode from the current season for $1.99 (as long as it has already aired on its network—they don't appear here until they have), and it downloads onto your computer, and then onto your iPod the next time you sync to your computer.

---

iTip: Downloading Multiple Episodes

When you download TV shows, they download in episode order so you can watch the shows in the same order they were broadcast. This might not matter as much with a comedy like The Office, *but it's very important for shows like* Lost *or* Grey's Anatomy, *where there is a continuing storyline from week to week.*

Downloading an Entire Season

If you want to download the entire current season of a show, then you'll probably want to buy a Season Pass (they vary in price, usually between $23.99 and $44.99). The advantages are: (a) you don't have to worry about falling behind—once an episode airs it will automatically be added to your Download queue so you can download each episode when you're ready to watch it; (b) it's convenient, because there's only one button to push, and you get every new episode of the season; and perhaps most importantly, (c) in some cases, it will save you money. For example, let's look at the CBS drama *CSI: Crime Scene Investigation*. A typical TV season runs between 20 and 25 shows. Let's go on the high end (*CSI* is usually closer to 25), and say there are 25 shows this season. Well, the Season Pass for *CSI* is $44.99, but if you bought them individually at $1.99 an episode, you'd spend $49.75. You're saving around $5 with the Season Pass. Not bad. Of course, the price (and amount of savings) varies from show to show, but it's pretty easy to do the math and see if you'll save money with a Season Pass. As I pointed out, though, that's not the only reason to buy a Season Pass. To buy a Season Pass, just click on the show you want to buy, and when you get to its page within the iTunes Store, click on the Buy Season Pass button. Some shows don't have a regular season, like E!'s *The Soup* or some specialized news shows, and those shows use a Multi-Pass instead, where you get a set number of shows for one price. Lastly, if a season is over, you can buy all the episodes by clicking the Buy Season button.

Choosing Which Videos Go onto Your iPod

By default, all your movies, TV shows, and podcasts will automatically be transferred to your iPod when you sync your iPod with your computer. That's fine if you bought a 160-GB iPod, but if you have a smaller capacity iPod (and video files are pretty huge), you might have to be pickier about which videos make it over to your iPod. To do that, connect your iPod to your computer, then click on the Movies tab (near the top of your main window). To choose exactly which movies make it onto your iPod (and which don't), click on the radio button for Selected movies, and from the list of movies that appear below it, only turn on the checkbox beside the movies you want copied onto your iPod, then click the Apply button in the bottom-right corner of the iTunes window. Now do the same thing for both the TV Shows tab and Podcasts tab.

---

iTip: Manually Managing Videos

Another way to control exactly which videos make it onto your iPod is to manage your iPod manually—so you literally drag-and-drop each individual movie, TV show, or music video you want right from iTunes onto your iPod. To switch to "Manual mode," just go to the Summary tab, and turn on the checkbox for Manually Manage Music and Videos.

Making Home Videos Play on Your iPod

Any videos you buy from the iTunes Store, or video podcasts you download from the iTunes Store, are already in the right format to play on your iPod. If you import other videos into iTunes (like home movies or free videos you've downloaded from the Web), chances are they'll play within iTunes with no problem, as iTunes supports all the same video formats that Apple's QuickTime video format does. So, what's the problem? The problem is your iPod doesn't support all those same formats. So, if you import a video into iTunes, when you sync your iPod, you'll get an error message along the lines of "This video cannot be played on your iPod." Don't sweat it—you just need to have iTunes convert that video to a video file format your iPod does support. You do that in iTunes by first clicking on the video in question, then going under the Advanced menu (up top) and choosing Convert Selection for iPod. That's it—it converts the video to a format your iPod supports, and now all you have to do is sync again, and the video is copied onto your iPod. See, that was easier than it sounds.

---

iTip: Importing Your Own Videos

Importing a "home-grown" video into iTunes is easy: just drag the video clip into the iTunes main window and it will import automatically. If, for some strange reason, that doesn't work, then just go under the iTunes File menu and choose Import.

Downloading Movies

Downloading movies into your iPod is as easy as downloading TV shows and music videos, but there are a few important differences. First click on the iTunes Store link in the Source list. On the Store's homepage, click on the Movies link in the top-left list of links to get to the main movie page. When you find a movie you're interested in, simply click on it to go to its page within the iTunes Store (the page for the comedy *Cars* is shown above). Besides the title and MPAA rating (PG, PG-13, R, etc.), these pages also include abbreviated lists of movie credits and offer a short plot summary. You can also click the round View Trailer button (or click on the movie poster) to view the full movie trailer right in the iTunes window. If you decide you want to buy the movie, click the Buy Movie button (movies are generally priced from $9.99 to $14.99). Now, here's the thing: movies have pretty huge file sizes, ranging anywhere from about 700+ MB to nearly 2 GB. So, you can plan on having them download for quite a while, even with a high-speed broadband Internet connection, but here's the good news: after they've been downloading for five minutes or so, you can actually start watching the movie, right there in iTunes, while it downloads the rest of the movie.

iTip: Search for Songs Only

The iPod's built-in Search feature (covered in a previous chapter) only searches for songs on your iPod—not movies, TV shows, or music videos.

Playing Your Downloaded Videos in iTunes

When you buy videos (TV shows, movies, etc.) from the iTunes Store, it downloads those videos onto your computer and into iTunes so you can access them easily (and copy them onto your iPod). However, another great feature is that you can actually watch these videos right from within iTunes itself. For example, let's say you downloaded an episode of the hit ABC show *Desperate Housewives*, and you'd like to watch it right now on your computer. All you have to do is click on TV Shows, under Library on the left side of the iTunes window, and a list of all the shows you've downloaded will appear. In that list, you'll see the episode of *Desperate Housewives*. Double-click on that listing and the show will begin to play in the tiny window in the lower-left corner of the iTunes window where you'd normally see album art. Now, if it seems kinda puny (and it will), then click directly on that tiny window and a much larger floating video window will appear (as shown above). If you move your cursor anywhere over this video window, a set of onscreen controls will appear near the bottom of the window with controls for pausing/playing the video, rewinding, fast forwarding, scrubbing through the video, and controlling the volume. On the far-right side of the onscreen controller are two diagonal arrows pointing outward. That's actually a button— click on it and your video then plays full screen. To return to the smaller floating video window, either press the Esc key on your keyboard, or move your cursor over the video and when the onscreen controller reappears, you can click on the same Full Screen button again (but now it looks like two inward-facing arrows).

Managing Your Downloads

When you buy a video from the iTunes Store, it starts downloading immediately, and a new link called Downloads is added to the Source list in the Store section, just below the link to your purchased items. Click on this link, and you'll see a list of all your downloads in progress (you can have up to three items downloading at once, and beyond that, other items will be listed there as waiting in the queue). Here's the cool thing: you can choose which order your items will be downloaded in by dragging them into the order you want, just like you'd drag items in a regular playlist. If you need to stop the downloading process and resume it later, just click the little Pause button that appears to the right of the status bar. To resume your download, click the circular button that now appears in its place. To resume all your downloads at once, click the Resume All button that appears in the bottom-right corner of the main window. By the way, once all your videos are downloaded, this Downloads link goes away.

---

iTip: Playing Videos Larger

If you'd always like to have any videos you watch within iTunes play in the much larger floating video window, then go to the iTunes Preferences, and in the Playback tab, in the middle, for Play Movies and TV Shows and Play Music Videos, choose In a Separate Window from the pop-up menus. If you always want your videos to play full screen, you can choose that from the pop-up menus, as well, and from then on you'll get the full-screen experience. Ahh, that's better.

Getting Your Videos onto Your iPod

Okay, so you've downloaded some movies, TV shows, and music videos, but now you want to get them onto your iPod so you can take the show on the road (get it? Show on the road? Come on, this stuff is gold!). Here's all you have to do: connect your iPod to your computer, iTunes will launch (if it's not already open), and it will automatically update your iPod with your newly downloaded videos. It's as easy as that. Connect it and it does the rest.

---

iTip: Be Sure You Want to Buy

When you click the Buy Episode, Buy Season Pass, Buy Multi-Pass button, etc., a friendly little dialog appears asking you if you're sure you want to buy the video. If you click Buy, that video is yours—forever. There is no additional Cancel button, no "Oh, I didn't mean to do that" button after that little warning dialog, and there are no returns. In short, pause for just a moment and make darn sure the video you're about to buy is the video you want to own, because my friend, that video is now officially yours.

Playing Videos on Your iPod classic

Once you've downloaded some videos and plugged your iPod into your computer (so the videos are downloaded onto your iPod), you can now watch them on the iPod's built-in color screen. From the main menu, scroll down and click on Videos. This brings up the main Videos menu with a list of the different kinds of videos you can play (Movies, TV Shows, or Music Videos). Scroll down to the type of video you want to watch. In this case, we'll watch that episode of *Desperate Housewives* we downloaded earlier, so scroll down to TV Shows and press the Select button. This brings up a list of the TV shows you've downloaded. Scroll down to the show you want to watch, press the Select button, and all the episodes of the show that you've downloaded will appear. Scroll to the episode you want to watch, press the Select button, and the show starts. So basically, once you're in the TV Shows menu, just find the show you want, find the episode you want, select it, and it plays. To pause the show, press the Play/Pause button on the Click Wheel. To resume it, press the Play/Pause button again. Movies and music videos work pretty much the same way—scroll to either Movies or Music Videos in the main Videos menu, find the movie title (or musical artist) you want, press the Select button, and it plays.

---

iTip: Pausing a Video

If you're watching a TV show, movie, or music video and stop or pause it, and then you come back to it later (even days later), it picks up right where you left off. See, it cares.

Controlling Your Video Playback

When you're playing videos, the controls on the iPod work in much the same way as when you're playing music. For example, to pause a video, press the Play/Pause button on the Click Wheel. To resume it, press the Play/Pause button again. If you click the Next/Fast-Forward button once, it jumps to the next video in your list, and clicking the Previous/Rewind button once jumps back to the beginning of the current video. If, instead of just clicking, you press-and-hold the Next/Fast-Forward button, it fast forwards through your video, and if you press-and-hold the Previous/Rewind button…well, you get the idea. Pressing the Menu button sends you back to the list of videos you were last in. To control the volume of your video, glide your finger clockwise around the Click Wheel to increase the volume, or counterclockwise to lower it (as soon as you start gliding your finger, a volume bar appears onscreen).

---

iTip: Click Video Controls

While playing a video, each time you press the center Select button, a new control appears: one click brings up time remaining, two clicks brings up a scrubber bar (for jumping forward or backward in the video), and three clicks brings up the Brightness control.

Importing Other Videos onto Your iPod

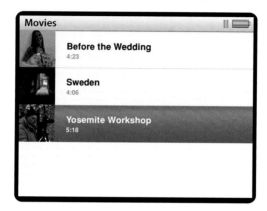

Besides the videos you buy online from the iTunes Store, you can watch other types of videos (like your home movies, for example, saved in QuickTime format), as long as they're in either MPEG-4 or H.264 format (luckily, these are two very popular formats for digital video). You just open iTunes, find those videos on your hard disk, then drag-and-drop them into the iTunes window, and they will be imported into iTunes. You'll find these newly imported videos by clicking on the Movies link in the iTunes Source list on the left side of the iTunes window. To play one of these movies in iTunes, just double-click on it in the list. To move these movies to your iPod, just connect your iPod to your computer, they'll be downloaded to your iPod, and you can find them in your Movies menu.

---

iTip: Converting Other Videos

What if you have video that you really want on your iPod, but it's not in MPEG-4 or QuickTime format? Then you need Apple's QuickTime 7 Pro software to convert it to iPod format. You can buy QuickTime 7 Pro (for Windows or Mac) from Apple.com. Once installed, just open the video file you want to convert (QuickTime Pro opens most popular video formats), then from the File menu choose Export. In the Export dialog, choose Movie to iPod, then click Save. Now you can drag that movie into iTunes.

Video Podcasts Aren't Under Videos

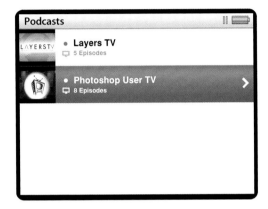

Your iPod treats video podcasts differently than movies, TV shows, and music videos in that video podcasts don't show up under the Videos menu—instead they have their own separate heading in the main menu. So, to see a video podcast, start at the main menu and choose Podcasts. This brings up a list of the different podcasts you've down-loaded, and if you click on a podcast and see a tiny TV screen icon to the left of an epi-sode's name, that lets you know it's a video podcast (at this point in time, the majority of podcasts are still audio podcasts, but video podcasts are growing in popularity by leaps and bounds, and more and more are released each day).

---

iTip: My Video Podcast

I'm the co-host of PhotoshopUser TV, *which is a free 30-minute weekly video podcast that I host with my buddies Dave Cross and Matt Kloskowski, where we share our favorite Adobe Photoshop tutorials and tips. We started this video podcast back in October 2005, and before that it was an audio podcast called* Photoshop Radio. *You can watch it right on our website at www.photoshopusertv.com, or by subscribing to it for free from the iTunes Store. Stop by and check it out if you get a chance.*

Watching iPod Videos on Your TV Screen

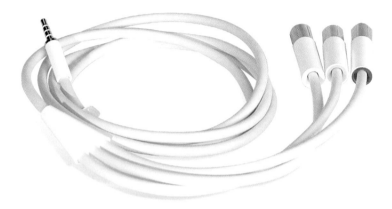

Want to watch the videos on your iPod on a much bigger screen (like your TV screen)? It's pretty darn simple, but it does require a Universal Dock (for newer iPods) and the Apple iPod AV Cable (available from Apple.com or your local Apple Store for $19), which connects your iPod to your TV. It's simple to use—connect the single plug to your universal Dock (for newer iPods) or your iPod's headphone jack (for fifth-generation or earlier iPods), then plug the two video and one audio cables into the AV jacks on your TV. One last thing: Go to your iPod's Videos menu, scroll down to Settings, and press the Select button. When the Video Settings menu appears, choose TV Out and press the Select button to change the setting from Off to On. Now when you play your video file on your iPod, it will play on your television as well, at full size. And because the videos in the iTunes Store are all now optimized for 640x480 resolution (the standard resolution for full-frame TV), the video looks great (nearly DVD quality).

---

iTip: Play Your Videos Remotely

Okay, want to take things up a notch? If you have Apple's Universal Dock (and the Apple AV Cable mentioned above or an S-video cable), then all you'd need to buy is the Apple Remote (see Chapter 13), which is a wireless controller for the Dock. Then, you simply put your iPod in the Universal Dock, connect the AV or S-video cable from the Line Out port on the Dock into your TV's inputs, then sit back with the remote and run the whole thing wirelessly from your couch. Sweet!

Watching iPod Videos on TV in Style

Apple's iPod AV Cable will certainly let you connect your iPod to your TV so you can watch videos on your television, but if you really want to do it up right, then you should check out Digital Lifestyle Outfitters' DLO HomeDock Deluxe. You just pop your iPod into this dock, connect the dock to your TV, then pick up the wireless remote that comes with it, and watch your videos, movies, and even video podcasts from the comfort of your easy chair (by the way, I'm not exactly sure what an "easy chair" is, but I'm pretty sure I don't have one). Of course, it also plays your music, as well, but one of the things I love about it is the built-in onscreen menus that let you choose just what you want to watch (or hear). I have one of these in my home, and I just love it. It's around $150 (DLO.com). You'll totally dig it (how do you like that 1970's lingo? I like to think of it as "retro throwback speak" in hopes that it will make a verbal resurgence).

---

iTip: Unplug Before Playing Videos

You can't play music or videos on your iPod while it is connected to your computer—you have to unplug your iPod first.

Putting Imported Music Videos Where They Belong

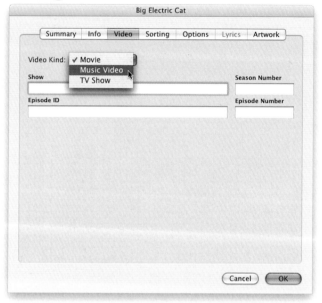

If you've downloaded some music videos from the Web (or, worse yet, you created your own homemade music video), you can drag-and-drop these MP4 videos into iTunes, but here's the thing—they won't show up under Music Videos. iTunes will see them as movies (after all, they are in the MP4 movie format), so it will put them in your Movies Library, right beside *Pirates of the Caribbean: The Curse of the Black Pearl* and *Gone in 60 Seconds*. However, it doesn't have to be that way. Once the video is imported, go to the Movies Library, find your imported music video, click on it, then press Command-I (PC: Ctrl-I) to bring up the clip's Get Info dialog (shown above). When it appears, click on the Video tab, and in the Video Kind pop-up menu, choose Music Video, then click OK. This will reclassify it as a music video, and now it will appear where it belongs—under your Music Video playlist and in your Music Library.

Burning Your Videos to DVD

Okay, that headline is a little misleading, because although you can back up your downloaded videos to DVD, you're only allowed (due to digital rights management issues) to burn your backup to a data DVD (a DVD that stores computer files), and not a standard DVD that plays in your television's DVD player. This is a key part of the copyright protection scheme that makes all this legal online downloading possible, so it's worth understanding and supporting. So, to back up your purchased movies and videos to a data DVD (provided, of course, that your computer has a DVD burner), just go under the File menu and choose Back Up to Disc. When the iTunes Backup dialog appears, you can choose exactly what you want to back up, and then click the Back Up button. It's going to ask you to insert a blank DVD, so go ahead (hey, why not) and it does all the dirty work for you. That's pretty much it. By the way, if you're moving these movies to another computer, or the unthinkable happens (your hard drive crashes, which is actually not unthinkable—it's more like inevitable), you just pop that DVD in, and iTunes will ask you if you want to restore the videos that are on that disc. Pretty well designed.

Moving Your Movies to Another Computer

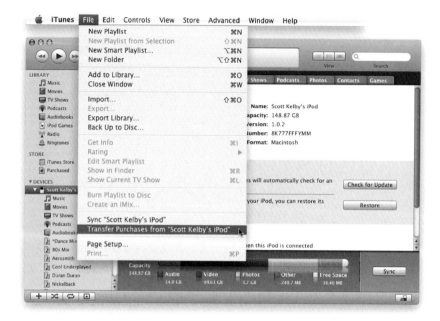

If you want to move movies and other videos from one computer to another, you can go the "Burn the Backup DVD" route shown on the previous page, but that's really for long-term backing up of your purchases. If you just want to transfer the videos you bought to another of your authorized computers (you're allowed to authorize up to five computers to play your purchased video and music contents from the iTunes Store), there's an easier way—just download the movies right from your iPod. Here's how it works: First, connect your iPod to the other computer you've authorized to play your music and videos. A dialog will appear asking you if you want to transfer your purchased videos and music to this other authorized computer (by the way, if it doesn't ask you, you can still have it do this by going under the File menu and choosing Transfer Purchases from Scott Kelby's iPod. Of course, yours won't say "Scott Kelby's iPod," unless your name is indeed Scott Kelby, in which case, I salute you). When you click OK, it takes over the task from there and copies your purchased videos and music onto your computer. Couldn't be easier or faster.

Stretching Your Battery Life Watching Movies

As you might imagine, playing a movie for 2+ hours is going to put some serious drain on your battery life, because the thing that eats up the most battery power is that gloriously bright full-color screen. So, if you're watching a 3-hour movie, and want to make sure you make it to the end of the movie without having to recharge (like when you're on a commercial flight), then simply press the center Select button three times to bring up the Brightness slider. When the Brightness slider appears, glide your finger counterclockwise around the Click Wheel to lower the brightness and extend your battery life (the darker you go—the longer your battery will last). *Note:* If you're not watching a video and want to change the Brightness settings, go under the iPod's Settings menu (from the main menu) to change the brightness.

---

iTip: How to Tell It's a Music Video

If you buy a music video from the iTunes Store, when it downloads into iTunes it appears in the Music Videos playlist but it also appears in your Music Library along with your audio files. So, how you do know which item in your Music Library is a song and which is a music video? If it's a music video, iTunes puts a little TV screen icon to the right of the item's name, so it stands out easily in your Music Library.

A Faster Way to Find Videos in the Store

If you go to the iTunes Store, and you know the name of the TV show or movie you're looking for, you can save yourself a lot of wasted time digging through the various menus until you find the video you're after if you just use the Search field at the top-right corner of the iTunes window. For example, if you're trying to find the TV show *Lost*, just go to the iTunes Store, and once it comes up, go right to the Search field and enter "Lost." It will instantly bring up every song, podcast, album, and video with "Lost" as a part of the title. Just glance in the TV Shows section and you'll find it right there—just one click away.

Broadcasting Movies from iTunes to Your TV

This isn't exactly an iPod thing, it's more of an iTunes thing, but since the two are so closely associated, I didn't think you'd mind my mentioning that Apple makes a very clever device called Apple TV, which lets you wirelessly broadcast the music, videos, TV shows, and movies on your iPod directly to your television set. You just connect your Apple TV to your television set (the 40-GB Apple TV is $299; the 160-GB model is $399. By the way, get the 160-GB model) and follow the onscreen instructions (it's simple). Once your Apple TV is up and running, its icon will appear in your Devices list (on the left side of the iTunes window), and iTunes it will automatically sync your music and movies to your Apple TV, just like it syncs with your iPod. Apple did a really brilliant job with the design and setup of the Apple TV, and once you have it, you'll wonder how you got along without it.

Chapter Seven
Get the Freeze-Frame
Using Your iPod's Photo Features

So, does this chapter win the award for "Most Obvious Chapter Title" or what? It's almost *too* obvious a name for a chapter about working with photos on your iPod, but I used it anyway, because besides being too obvious, it's also too perfect. By the way (*Warning:* Quick iPod history lesson coming), there was a time when iPods only played music. In fact, for a while there was only one model of iPod that even supported the viewing of photos. It was called (are you ready for this) the "iPod photo." Its name was almost as obvious as the name of this chapter. Now, why does all this matter? It matters plenty, because although book editors don't read the introductions of books any more, they do read these chapter intros. These people are really picky, and insist on seeing things in these chapter intros like long words and punctuation. They also like it if I can work in a French word or two, because then they get to use their French dictionary and apparently they get some kind of kickback or bonus when that happens. Plus, they love to casually mention it in front of other editors: "I was working on Scott's book today, and I would have been done sooner, but I had to keep loading the French dictionary." The other editors all look at each other and go, "Oooooh. French!" So basically, I do it for them. They have so little, so if I toss in a long word here (like ostensively), and a French phrase there (like *Mon oreille est un bouton de porte*), then they'll let lots of other stuff slip by. Like this intro, for example.

119

Mac: Importing Photos from Apple's iPhoto

If you're a Mac user, the easiest way to get your photos from your Mac onto your iPod is to use Apple's iPhoto application (which has come preinstalled on every Mac for about as long as I can remember). If you're already using iPhoto for storing your images, you can just plug your iPod into your computer for syncing, and any photos you've imported into iPhoto will automatically be copied onto your iPod (if you're not using iPhoto yet, you'll find it in your Mac's Applications folder). Launch iPhoto and then drag any photos on your computer right into iPhoto's main window to import them. Once they're imported, you can create individual albums (kind of like playlists, but for photos instead of music), which are supported by your iPod. By default, it wants to import all your photos and albums, but if you prefer to have just specific albums of photos copied over to your iPod, first connect your iPod to your computer, then in iTunes, click on the Photos tab. Next, under Sync Photos From, click on the Selected Albums radio button, and in the list below, turn on the checkbox beside each album you want copied onto your iPod. Now press the Apply button in the bottom-right corner. The first time you do this, you might want to get comfy, 'cause this could take a while. Luckily, you only have to do this once. From then on, it'll just import any new photos you add to, or delete any photos you remove from, iPhoto (if you imported all photos) or the albums you specified.

Mac: Importing Photos from a Folder

If you don't want to use Apple's iPhoto for getting your photos over to your iPod (or for some reason you don't have iPhoto), you can just put your photos in a folder. (*Note:* If you create subfolders inside that main folder, they'll be imported into your iPod as separate albums, as if you were using iPhoto. Cool, eh?) Once your photos are in a folder, connect your iPod to your computer, then once it appears in iTunes, click on the Photos tab. At the top, there's a pop-up menu for Sync Photos From, and from that menu, select Choose Folder. A standard Open dialog will appear, so navigate to your folder of images and click the Choose button. Now, just click the Apply button in the bottom-right corner of the iTunes window and your images in that folder (and in any subfolders you created within it) will be uploaded to your iPod.

Windows PC: Importing Photos from Photoshop Elements

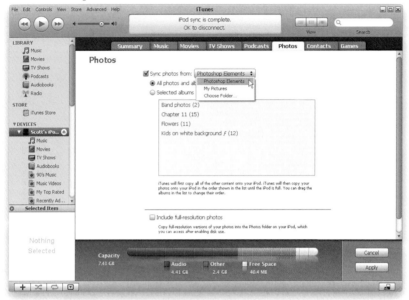

If you're using a PC, the easiest way to get your photos onto your iPod is to use either Adobe Photoshop Album Starter Edition (free from Adobe at www.adobe.com/products/ photoshopalbum/starter.html) or Photoshop Elements, which has a very robust photo organizer built right in, as well as amazing image-editing controls, for around $100. Once your photos are organized in either Album or Elements, the next step is to connect your iPod to your computer. Then, once your iPod appears in the Source list on the left side, click on the Photos tab. When the Photos tab appears, turn on the Sync Photos From checkbox, and from the pop-up menu, choose Photoshop Album Starter (or Photoshop Elements, if you're using that). Just below that menu, you can choose whether you want to import every single photo you have (in an album) or just specific images (or albums). If you choose the All Photos and Albums route, once you click Sync or Apply, you can take a lunch break because it could easily take an hour or more to import all your photos. Luckily, you only have to do this once. From then on, it'll just import any new photos you add, or delete any photos you remove.

Windows PC: Importing Photos from a Folder

If you're using a PC and you don't have either Adobe Photoshop Elements or Adobe Photoshop Album for getting your photos over to your iPod, you can just put your photos inside a folder within your My Pictures folder (*Note:* If you create subfolders inside your new folder, they'll be imported into your iPod as separate collections, as if you were using Elements or Album). Once your photos are in a folder, connect your iPod to your computer, then once it appears in iTunes, click on the Photos tab in the main window. At the top, there's a pop-up menu for Sync Photos From, and from that menu, select Choose Folder. A standard Browse for Folder dialog will appear, so first navigate to your My Pictures folder, then find the folder with your photos, click on it to select it, then click the OK button. Now just click the Apply button in the bottom-right corner of the iTunes window and your images in that folder (and in any subfolders you created within it) will be uploaded to your iPod.

How to Import Just Specific Photo Albums

By default, when you connect your iPod to your computer, it wants to import every single photo you have in your iPhoto library (or on your PC, your Photoshop Album Starter Edition or Photoshop Elements collection, or any subfolders within your My Pictures folder). This can take, well…it seems like forever, but it's probably only an hour or so. You can speed up this process by importing only the specific albums you want imported. That way, only your favorite photos are copied onto your iPod, and not *every* photo you have. To do this, connect your iPod to your computer, launch iTunes, and click on the Photos tab in the iPod Preferences window. Then click on the Selected Albums (or Selected Folders, depending on your Sync Photos From choice) radio button. In the area below, turn on the checkbox beside each album you want imported. Now, only those albums will be imported, saving you lots of time (and space on your iPod).

---

iTip: Create Separate Folders

You don't have to use Photoshop Album or Photoshop Elements to create separate collections of your photos. Just create separate folders inside your My Pictures folder. Name each folder with the name you want for a collection, and then drag the photos you want to appear in each collection into the corresponding folder. Then when you import photos from your My Pictures folder, any folders inside the My Pictures folder will import as separate collections that you can access from the Photos menu on your iPod.

Viewing Photos You've Imported

Once you've copied your photos over onto your iPod, viewing them is easy. From the main menu, scroll down to Photos, then press the Select button. Any albums of photos you've imported will then appear in a list. To see the photos in a particular album, scroll to that album, then press the Select button again and tiny thumbnails of the photos in that album will appear. The first thumbnail will have a yellow high-light around it. To see that photo, just press the Select button again and that photo will now appear full-screen size. To get back to the thumbnails again, press the Menu button, and now you can use the Click Wheel to scroll to a different thumbnail, and click on it to see it full screen. To see the next photo at full-screen size, press the Next/ Fast-Forward button. To see the previous photo, press the Previous/Rewind button. To scroll quickly through your images at full-screen size, just glide around the Click Wheel clockwise (to move quickly forward) or counterclockwise (to move quickly back to the beginning of that album).

Seeing a Photo Slide Show

PHOTO BY SCOTT KELBY

To see a slide show of your photos, start at the main menu, scroll down and click on Photos, then click on the photo album you want to see as a slide show, and press the Play/Pause button. To pause a running slide show, press the Play/Pause button (to restart it, just press Play/Pause again). To quit the slide show and return to your list of albums, press the Menu button. Also, if you're scrolling through your thumbnails, you can start a slide show from any thumbnail by just pressing the Play/Pause button, and your slide show will start with that photo.

Customizing Your Slide Show

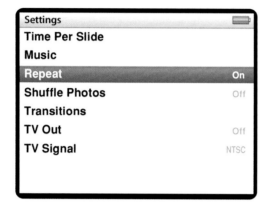

Your iPod gives you a surprisingly robust amount of control over how (and where) your slide show is displayed. To find these controls, start at the main menu, scroll down and click on Photos, then scroll down and click on Settings for a list of slide show options. We'll cover adding music and setting the duration of each slide on the next two pages, but there are other options here worth mentioning. For example, you can scroll down to Repeat and press the Select button to have your slide show loop back to the beginning and start over when it's done, or click Shuffle Photos to have the photos appear in a random order. The Transition preference lets you choose what happens between slides to reveal the next slide (personally, I like the Cross Fade, which is kind of a dissolve effect), but you can choose any one you'd like (the default setting is Random). If you want a "cut" (one slide replaces the other with no transition between), choose None. If you want to show your slide show on TV (you're using Apple's Composite or Component AV Cable to connect your iPod to your television), once you've connected your iPod to your TV's video and audio jacks, scroll down to TV Out, press the Select button, and set it to On or Ask. Now press Menu to jump back to your list of albums, click on the one you want to see as a slide show, then press the Play/Pause button.

Adding Music to Your Slide Show

If there's one thing a slide show definitely needs, it's a music track playing behind it. You can add music in one of two ways—you can assign a song in iPhoto, then that song plays automatically when you play that slide show on your iPod. If you'd prefer to choose your background music "on the fly," go to the iPod's main menu, click on Photos, click on Settings, then click on Music, and select which playlist you'd like to play during the slide show. Now you can start your slide show.

iTip: Getting a Single Song

Even though in iPhoto you can pick either a single song or a playlist, in the iPod you can only pick a playlist. The only way to get a single song in the iPod is to select a playlist that only has one song in it.

Changing the Duration of Each Slide

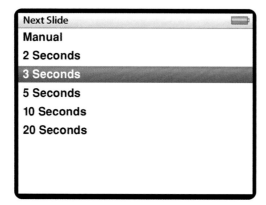

By default, each slide will remain on your iPod screen for 3 seconds. If you'd like each photo to remain onscreen longer (or shorter, for that matter), just start at the main menu, click on Photos, click on Settings, then click on Time Per Slide and choose from the list of times.

---

iTip: Turn Off Auto-Launch

If you're using your iPod to store files or backups, having iTunes launch each time you connect your iPod can be incredibly irritating. What's worse is if you're connecting your iPod as a hard drive to another computer, iTunes will automatically sync with that computer. Luckily, you can turn off this "auto iTunes launch" by connecting your iPod to your computer, and from the Summary page in the iPod Preferences window, turn off the checkbox for the Open iTunes When This iPod Is Connected option and click Apply. That's it—no more auto-launch.

Using Your iPod for Presentations

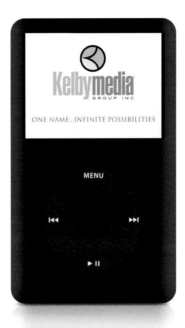

Want to really "tune up" the crowd at your next business presentation? Instead of lugging your laptop to the conference room and hooking up a projector, just bring along your iPod and Apple's Composite or Component AV Cable (older iPods can use the Apple AV Cable), and you can just connect your iPod directly to the projector. Instead of showing photos, show a slide presentation of your album and use the iPod's Next/Fast-Forward button to advance to the next "slide." Of course, you can even have music behind your slide presentation. If you really want to take things up a notch, get the Apple (iPod) Remote, so you can stand at the front of the room and control your iPod (advancing it through your presentation slides), while it sits quietly back there by the projector.

iTip: Knowing What Comes Next

While in Slideshow mode, you can see your next photo on the iPod screen before everyone else. This is cool for doing presentations and knowing which photo or slide is coming up next.

Seeing Your Slide Show on TV

To see your slide show on TV, use the Apple Composite or Component AV Cable to connect your iPod to the inputs on your TV. (*Note:* Older iPods can use the Apple AV Cable.) Put the thin, single plug into the headphone jack on the top of your iPod, then insert the audio and video connectors into the input jacks on your TV. (*Note:* If you're a freak for high-quality image display, you can use an S-video connector with any model iPod to connect to your TV instead. To use S-video, you'll have to place your iPod into its Dock, then attach an S-video cable to the S-video output on the back of the Dock, and connect the other end to your TV's S-video input.) Once connected, from the main menu, click on Photos, then scroll down and click on Settings. Scroll to TV Out and click the Select button until it changes to Ask. Now, scroll to the photo album you want to display as a slide show, then press the center Select button, scroll to the photo you want to start with, and press the center Select button again. Once your full-screen image appears, press the Select button, which brings up the screen shown above, and you can use the Click Wheel to slide the blue button to On, which sets your iPod to display on a TV. Now press the center Select button to begin your "big-screen" experience. (*Note:* If you connect your iPod Dock via the S-video cable, you also need to connect the line out to your TV or stereo speakers via an audio cable. The included TV cables *only* work from the headphone jack on top of the iPod.)

Getting Your Stored Photos onto Your Computer

If you've backed up a bunch of photos (or other files) onto your iPod, and now you want to transfer them to another computer so you can edit them, sort them, and if you like, transfer them from that computer back to your iPod, here's how to do just that: Connect your iPod to your computer, then go to iTunes. When iTunes launches, you'll see your iPod listed in the Source list on the left side of the iTunes window. In the iPod Preferences window, in the Options section, turn on the checkbox for Enable Disk Use. Once you do this, the iPod will appear on your computer as a mounted disk (like a hard disk or USB device). Go to your computer's desktop, double-click on the now-visible iPod, and you'll see the folder with your stored photos (don't disturb the folder named Photos). Now you can select these photos and drag them onto your computer.

Chapter Eight
iTouch Myself
Using the iPod touch

▶▶ Before we get started, I just want you to know that I'm fully aware that: (a) the real name of the song by The DiVinyls is "I Touch Myself" and not "iTouch Myself," but it just seemed so obvious a tie-in that I had to do it; and (b) I know that the title is a little naughty, but as any book publisher will tell you, working naughty things into your book is really what ultimately sells the book. It's not the step-by-step instructions or helpful tips that make your life easier. As my editor says, "That stuff is for suckers." In fact, oftentimes I'll submit a chapter, and my editor will call me (we'll call him "Ted" because that's his real name), and Ted will say something along the lines of "Do you want this book to sell? Then you'd better 'sex it up' a bit." So I go back to those chapters and I try to insert what I believe to be totally innocent words, but for which people with naughty minds (not you) apparently insert their own meanings. Now, because you're not one of these people, you totally won't get how these words could possibly be misconstrued as "dirty," but rest assured, "those" people will find a way. Here's a perfect example: melons. See, it's just a fruit commonly sold at every grocery store, but "those" people assign some sort of twisted meaning to it. Pickle. See, another innocent grocery store item (much like sausage or wiener), but Ted insists I put these in, including the occasional lurid poultry reference, like thighs and breasts (I don't know about you, but I'm getting hungry). I'm sorry you had to be exposed to this seamy underbelly of publishing, but I thought you'd rather hear it from me, instead of picking it up on the streets.

Turning Your iPod touch On (and Putting It to Sleep)

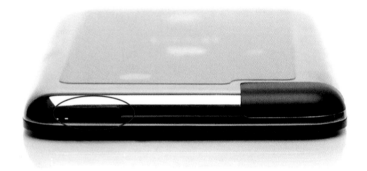

Turning on your iPod touch is easy: just press-and-hold the Sleep/Wake button located on the top of the iPod touch. The Apple logo will appear for a few moments, and then you'll see the Home screen. If you want to put your iPod touch to sleep (which is a great way to conserve battery life when you're not actively using any of its functions), you just press the Sleep/Wake button on the top once. When you put it to sleep, you'll hear a little click sound and your screen will go black. While your iPod touch is in this sleep mode, the buttons on the touch screen are deactivated, so if you toss it in your pocket (or purse) it won't accidentally come on and start playing a song, or a video, or doing anything that would run down the battery. To wake your iPod touch from sleep, you can either press that Sleep/Wake button again or press the Home button on the bottom center (just below the touchscreen). When it wakes, the screen is still locked (just in case you awakened it accidentally). To unlock the screen, just press your finger on the gray arrow button onscreen, slide it to the right, and the Home screen appears.

Turning Your iPod touch Off

If you want to turn your iPod touch completely off, just press-and-hold the Sleep/Wake button on the top of the iPod touch for a few seconds until the red Slide to Power Off button appears. To shut down, take your finger, press lightly on that red button, and just slide it to the right. Your screen will turn black and you'll see a small round status icon for just a moment, then your iPod touch will power off. If you somehow got to this "power down" screen by accident, just tap the Cancel button.

Using the Home Screen

PHOTO BY SCOTT KELBY

The Home screen is your main screen and the launching point for all of your iPod touch's features. In fact, this screen is so important that the only other "hard" button (besides the Sleep/Wake button on top) is the Home button, which is that round indented button just below the touchscreen on the face of your iPod touch. Anytime you press that button, it takes you to the Home screen. Once you're at the Home screen, the buttons at the top are for using the different applications that come with your iPod (like the Safari Web browser, access to YouTube videos, a calendar), and there's a Settings button to access your iPod's preferences. The standard iPod features (for playing music, videos, photos, or downloading music wirelessly from the iTunes Store) are those four buttons along the bottom of the Home screen. To use any one of these iPod features, just tap your finger once on the button. For example, if you wanted to look for some music, you'd just tap once on the Music button to enter the music section of your iPod touch.

Making Your Way Around

At the bottom of the main iPod touch Music screen is a navigation bar that, by default, gives you one-tap access to your Playlists, Artists, Songs, Albums, and there's a More button to take you to all the other music areas within your iPod. You can customize this little navigation bar so your favorite areas are there (for example, let's say you rarely view your music by artist, but you do watch a lot of podcasts—you could replace Artists with Podcasts, so you're just one click away from your list of podcasts. To do that, tap once on the More button, then when the More screen appears, tap the dark blue Edit button in the top-left corner of the touchscreen. This lists all the one-tap buttons available to you. Press-and-hold the Podcasts button to select it, slide that button directly down right onto the Artists button, and then remove your finger, and your Artists button is replaced with your Podcasts button. You're basically dragging-and-dropping. (You can also reorder these icons the same way.) That's how easy it is to customize your iPod's navigation bar.

---

iTip: No Replacing the More Button

The one button it won't let you replace is the More button, because if you were to replace it, you wouldn't be able to get back to that customization screen again, or any of the other buttons for that matter.

Playing a Song

To play a song, from the Home screen, tap on Music, then tap on Songs on the bottom navigation bar. Scroll to the song you want (by "flicking" upward on the touchscreen), simply tap the song's name, and it displays the cover art full screen (as shown above) and starts playing the song. A set of controls will appear near the bottom of the cover art, with a Rewind button (two left-facing arrows), Play/Pause button (the triangle or double lines) and a Fast-Forward button (two right-facing arrows). There's also a volume slider (at the bottom of the screen) that lets you control the volume—just press the little volume knob and slide it with your finger (slide to the right to increase the volume, left to lower the volume). To fast forward, press-and-hold the Fast-Forward button, and it will soon start to fast forward through your song. To jump to the next song in the list, just tap the Fast-Forward button once instead (the Rewind button works the same way: press-and-hold to rewind, or tap it once to play the current song again).

---

iTip: When There's No Cover Art

If you choose to play a song that doesn't have its own cover art, your iPod substitutes a fake cover with a large musical note (actually, it's a couple of eighth notes, but who's counting), which really makes you appreciate cover art.

How Many Songs Are on Your iPod touch?

To find out how many songs are on your iPod touch, press the Home button, then tap on the Settings button. In the Settings screen, tap on General, then tap on About, and it will list the total number of songs, videos, and photos that are on your iPod, and the amount of space still available (unused space left for adding more songs, videos, and photos) is listed there as well. If you want to see how many songs are in a particular playlist, tap on that playlist, and then scroll down to the bottom of the list of songs, where it will display how many songs are in that playlist (as shown above). However, if you have less than 20 songs in your playlist, then I guess your iPod figures there's so few you can just count 'em yourself, because it doesn't display the number. Not until you actually get 20 songs does it start displaying the number of songs in that playlist.

---

iTip: Scroll Using the Alphabet

When you're scrolling through long song lists of playlists, you can jump right to songs beginning with a specific letter by tapping your finger once on the letter in the vertical alphabetical list of letters on the right side of your list. If you don't see this vertical list, you don't have enough songs in that playlist for your iPod to display the "jump-to" alphabet. Also, you can press-and-hold your finger on this list and just slide up or down to quickly scroll through the list alphabetically.

Scrubbing, Repeating, and Shuffling

Once a song is playing, you can scrub through the song (drag the playhead forward or backward in a song) by tapping on the center of the screen, and a little scrubby slider will appear near the top of the screen. Use your finger to drag the little playhead forward or backward (this is a great tool if you're trying to figure out the words to a song. As soon as a lyric goes by, you can scrub back just a little bit and hear it again, and repeat that as many times as you'd like until you realize it's saying "'scuse me while I kiss the sky" instead of "'scuse me while I kiss this guy"). Besides scrubbing, there are two other important controls that appear on either side of this scrubby slider: (1) On the left of the slider is the Repeat button. If you tap on it once, it turns blue (to let you know repeat is turned on), and it will repeat your current playlist of songs. If you tap the Repeat button again, a tiny "1" now appears on the button, letting you know that it will now repeat just the current song again and again until you turn it off. And, (2) on the right side is the Shuffle button. Tap once to turn it on, and it shuffles the songs currently chosen (playing them in a random order). Tap it again to turn Shuffle off. Tap the center of the screen to hide the scrubby slider and the Repeat and Shuffle buttons. By the way, while you're playing a song, after just a few seconds your iPod's screen goes to sleep to help save battery life. To reawaken your iPod, just press the indented Home button, and then slide the unlock slider bar to the right.

Seeing the Other Songs on an Album

When you play a song in iTunes, the album cover art appears full screen, and if you want to see other songs you've downloaded from that same album, all you have to do is tap on the little icon in the top-right corner of the title bar (to the right of the song's name), and a list of other songs on your iPod from that same album will now appear, including each song's length and the star rating of the currently selected song (as seen above). To play one of those other songs, just tap on it. To see another album's songs, tap the Fast-Forward button, and each time you tap it, a new album of songs appears (if you only see one song listed, you have only downloaded one song from that album). To return to the normal Cover Art view, just tap on a blank area of the screen twice (do a double-tap). To return to the regular Songs list, tap the Back arrow button in the top-left corner of the screen.

---

iTip: Rating Songs in an Album List

If you see a song in this album list view that doesn't have a star rating, you can add one right then and there. Just tap on the little rating dots up top to add a rating (so, if you wanted to rate it four stars, you'd tap on the fourth little dot, and it changes to four stars). You can also press-and-slide your finger left or right to remove or add more stars. The next time you sync your iPod with your computer, these ratings you applied to songs on your iPod will get added to those same songs in your computer's iTunes.

Accessing Your Playlists

The playlists you create in iTunes are copied over to your iPod touch when you sync, and to see them (and hear them) on your iPod, tap on the Music icon (from the Home screen), then tap once on Playlists in the navigation bar at the bottom of the screen. This brings up your list of playlists (by default, iTunes copies all your playlists from your computer's copy of iTunes onto your iPod, but you can set things up so only certain playlists are copied over—see "Turning Off iPod Auto-Updating" in Chapter 4 for how to set that up). When you see a playlist you'd like to hear, tap once on it, then the songs in that playlist are displayed. Tap on any song in that list and it starts playing. The rest of the songs that follow in that playlist will now play in order.

---

iTip: Shuffling Your Playlist

At the very top of each playlist is a listing called Shuffle. Tap on it, and it immediately starts playing that playlist in a random order.

Instant Playlists of Your Favorite Artists

I have a number of playlists on my iPod that are dedicated to just one artist (for example, I have a James Taylor playlist of just my favorite JT songs, so when I'm in a mellow mood, I can hear just those songs). However, if you don't have a playlist for your favorite artists, that shouldn't stop you. In the main Music screen, in the bottom navigation bar, tap on Artists and a list of all the artists you have in your iPod appears. Scroll to the artist you'd like to hear (for example, let's say you want to hear all the Nickelback songs on your iPod), tap on Nickelback and you'll see a list of albums represented by the Nickelback songs you've downloaded. If you just want to hear all your Nickelback songs, regardless of which album they're on, tap on All Songs at the top of the list, and it does the rest. If you'd only prefer to hear one song from a particular album, then just tap on one of those albums in the list to see a listing of all the songs you've downloaded from that particular album. Then tap on the song you want to hear from that list, and it plays. You can also shuffle the songs on any album (so you don't hear them in the same order every time, like with a CD or traditional vinyl record album—at least, so I hear).

Making On-The-Go Playlists on an iPod touch

Creating an "On-The-Go" playlist (a playlist you create right on your iPod) is much different on an iPod touch than it is on any other iPod—it's a much more visual experience.
From the Home screen, start by tapping once on the Music button, then tap on Playlists,
and at the top of the list of playlists, you'll see On-The-Go. Tap on On-The-Go once, and
a list of all the songs on your iPod touch will appear. To the right of each song will be a +
(plus sign) button (as seen above), which you tap to add that song to your On-The-Go
playlist. When you're done, tap the Done button in the upper-right corner. From now
on, when you tap on On-The-Go in the Playlists list, it will display a list of the songs
in your On-The-Go playlist. To add more songs to this list, tap the Edit button in the
top-right corner, then tap the + (plus sign) button in the top left, and that list of all your
songs (with the plus sign beside them) will appear again—just tap the + (plus sign) button beside any songs you want to add (if a song has the plus sign beside it grayed out, it
means that song is already in your On-The-Go playlist), then tap the Done button.

Visual Searching by Album Cover

PHOTO BY SCOTT KELBY

The iPod touch has the same Cover Flow feature that iTunes itself has, where you can visually scroll through your entire music collection by cover art. To do this, just turn your iPod touch sideways (so the screen is horizontal), and it automatically enters the Cover Flow view. To move through the covers, just swipe your finger horizontally across the screen and the covers flow by in the direction you're "flicking." To stop the flowing, stop swiping. To view the songs on a particular album, just tap on it and the cover flips over to show you the songs you've downloaded from that album. Tap on any song to play it (when it's done, if there are other songs on that album, it'll play those, too). To return to the Cover Flow view, just tap twice in an open area. (*Note:* Your music doesn't stop playing—the view just changes back to Cover Flow.)

Watching Videos on Your iPod touch

If you've downloaded any video podcasts (or TV shows or movies, for that matter), you can watch any one of them by starting at the Home screen (you can return to the Home screen any time by pressing the round indented Home button that appears just below the touchscreen). Then tap once on Videos, and the main video screen will appear, and all the videos on your iPod touch will appear organized into categories by type (TV Shows, Movies, Podcasts, and Music Videos). To watch a video, scroll down and find it in the list, then tap on it and it begins playing. Videos play horizontally, so you'll want to turn your iPod touch sideways when watching videos. Once your video is playing, to see the controls for pausing, fast forwarding, rewinding, and volume, just tap anywhere on the screen and the controls will appear near the bottom of the screen. A scrubber bar also appears across the top of the screen—just press-and-hold your finger on the knob, and drag to the right to scrub forward in your video or drag left to scrub backward.

---

iTip: Toggling Between Video Modes

The iPod touch has two video modes: Cinematic, which displays your video in a wide-screen view more like the original theatrical presentation, so you'll see your video in "letterbox" view with thin black bars at the top and bottom of the screen. There's also Full Screen view, which zooms in so your video fills the screen. To toggle between these two modes, just tap twice on the screen.

Deleting Videos from Your iPod touch

Your iPod touch is the only iPod that lets you actually delete something (in this case, a video) from right within the iPod itself (normally, you can only delete songs, videos, or photos within Apple's iTunes application). To delete a video, find the video on your iPod's video list, then take your finger, press it on the right side of the video listing, and drag your finger back to the left. This reveals a red Delete button on the right side of the listing. Tap that button to delete the video and make more room for stuff like downloaded songs from the Wi-Fi iTunes Music Store.

---

iTip: Playing Audiobooks

Like any other iPod, the iPod touch can play audiobooks you've downloaded, and one nice feature (mentioned earlier in the book) is that you can listen to your audiobook on your iPod, and when you sync it with your computer, it tells iTunes the exact spot where you paused, so you can pick up listening to the book on your computer. If you pause the book in iTunes, when you resync your iPod touch, it tells your Touch where you left off.

Have Your iPod Sing You to Sleep

The iPod touch has a great sleep timer feature, which shuts down your iPod after a specific amount of time has passed. Here's how it works: Start at the Home screen, then tap on Clock. When the Clock main screen appears, tap on Timer in the bottom navigation bar. When the Timer screen appears (shown above), choose how long you want your iPod to play music before it puts itself to sleep by swiping your finger up and down to move the number wheels. Once you've set the amount of time (let's say 30 minutes, for example), then tap on the phrase "When Timer Ends" and a list of choices appears. Tap once on Sleep iPod, then tap the blue Set button in the top-right corner of the screen. Now tap the large green Start button, and 30 minutes later your music will gently fade out and your iPod will put itself to sleep (just like a sleep timer on an alarm clock radio).

Using the Other iPod touch Clock Features

There are three other clock features on the iPod touch. First, tap on World Clock (which lets you display the time in different time zones). To delete the default city, tap the Edit button in the top-left corner, then tap the red – (minus sign) button that appears before the city's name. This reveals a red Delete button to the right of the clock. Tap it once to delete that city/time zone. To add new cities, tap the + (plus sign) button in the top-right corner. This brings up the iPod touch's keyboard, where you can type in the city whose time zone you want to display. As you start typing the first few letters, it starts listing cities that start with those letters, so finding cities is quick and easy. When you find one you want (for example, Sydney, Australia), tap on it, and the clock is created. If the face of the clock is white, it's daytime in that city. If it's black, it's night. Now tap the Alarm button at the bottom of the screen. To set an alarm, press the + (plus sign) button in the top-right corner, and a list of options appears, where you choose to repeat it one day a week or every day. You can choose the alarm sound (tap the Sound field), whether you want a snooze option, and what you want to name your alarm. Below that, you choose the time in the same way you chose the sleep timer time on the previous page. If you tap Save, it adds an alarm to your list (you can create multiple alarms). Lastly, there's a Stopwatch feature that is incredibly simple—tap the green Start button to start timing, tap the red Stop button to stop it, tap the gray button for a Lap, and do I really have to tell you what the Reset button does?

Using the Built-In Keyboard

Anytime you need to type something on your iPod touch, a keyboard automatically appears onscreen. If the keys look kind of small, that's only because they are. Luckily, Apple has some features that make using the keyboard a lot easier. As you type onscreen, a large version of the letter you just typed pops up in front of your fingers so you can see instantly if you hit the right letter. I can tell you from experience that the more you use this keyboard, the easier it gets, so if you wind up misspelling just about every word when you first start—don't sweat it—in just a couple of days you'll be misspelling only every third to fourth word. There's also a pretty clever "auto-complete" function. Although it will suggest a word while you're typing it, go ahead and finish the word (especially if you've spelled it wrong) and it will replace your misspelled word with the correct word (95% of the time). You do have to get used to typing a word, seeing that you've misspelled it, and continuing to type. If you do that—you'll be amazed at how quickly you'll be able to type using this keyboard.

---

iTip: Fixing Typos

If you need to go back and fix a typo that the auto-complete feature didn't catch, just press-and-hold approximately where the typo occurred, and a magnifying Loupe appears onscreen so you can not only clearly see the location of your cursor, but you can move the cursor with your finger, as well, to quickly fix the mistake.

Getting Internet Access

When you're thinking of surfing the Web, you first need to be thinking, "Where can I find a wireless connection?" That's because, unlike Apple's iPhone (which uses AT&T's EDGE wireless network, so you can jump on the Web anywhere), the iPod touch needs to access a Wi-Fi network (like the public high-speed wireless hotspots at places like Starbucks, McDonalds, many hotel lobbies, etc., or you can jump on your office or home wireless connection) to connect to the Internet. When you tap on the Safari Web browser on the Home screen, your iPod touch immediately searches for an Internet connection, and if it sees a wireless network, it offers you the opportunity to try to access it. If it's a private, password-protected network, you'll see a padlock icon beside the network's name. If you don't know the password, you're not getting on. If it's an Open network (open to the public), then you won't see the padlock icon, and you can just tap on the network and you're connected.

Using the Safari Web Browser

Once you've got a wireless connection, you use the Safari Web browser to visit web-pages. There's a field at the top of Safari where you enter the Web address (URL) of the site you want to visit, so tap once on that field and the keyboard appears at the bottom of the screen. Type in the Web address of the site you want to visit, then press the blue Go button in the bottom-right corner. Once the webpage appears, you can get a wider, larger view by turning your iPod touch sideways. If you tap twice on any part of the webpage, it zooms in and has that area fill your screen. To zoom back out, tap twice on the screen again. You use your finger to scroll up/down and side-to-side on the page. To use a link you see on a webpage, just tap on it. To save the page as a bookmark, scroll up to the top of the page and tap the + (plus sign) button to the left of the address field. To reload the page, tap the circle button to the right of the address field. To erase the exist-ing address (so you can type in a new one), tap on the little gray X on the far right side of the address field. To go to a previously viewed page, tap the Left Arrow button at the bottom of the screen.

---

iTip: Using the ".com" Button

A lot of people don't notice this at first, but at the bottom of the keyboard, to the left of the blue Go button, is a ".com" button, and one tap on it types in ".com" for you, which is incredibly handy when entering URLs into Safari.

Using the Built-In Google Search

You don't have to go to Google.com to do a Web search, because it's built right into the Safari browser. In Safari, just tap on the URL address field, and you'll notice that two fields actually appear: the address field, and just below it a Google search field. So, if you know the URL you want, use the top field. If you don't, type in the search term in the second field. If you change your mind, tap the Cancel button up top.

---

iTip: Changing Search Engines

If you don't want to use Google as your built-in search engine, you can choose Yahoo! instead by going to the Home screen, then tapping on Settings, and in the Settings screen, tapping on Safari. When the Safari settings screen appears, tap once on Search Engine and it brings up a screen where you can change your search provider by tapping on Yahoo!

Working with Multiple Webpages

If you're on one webpage and you tap a link to visit another page, that page might be set up to open in a separate window (which is no problem—a new window will open to display that page). So now, you have multiple webpages open in Safari, and to see the various pages you have open, tap once on the little Pages button in the bottom-right corner. This shrinks the current page down to a smaller thumbnail size, and now you can scroll through the thumbnails of any open pages by swiping your finger left and right. To close one of these pages, just tap the red X in the upper-left corner of the thumbnail.

---

iTip: Accessing Bookmarks

If you've saved any sites as bookmarks, you can access your bookmark list by tapping once on the Bookmarks button (it looks like an open book) at the bottom-right side of your Safari screen. This brings up a list of your bookmarked sites, and to visit one of those, just tap on it in the list.

Importing Bookmarks from Your Computer

You can have the bookmarks on your computer automatically copied over to your Safari Web browser on your iPod touch, but you have to turn this feature on. First, connect your iPod touch to your computer for syncing, and then when it appears in iTunes, click on the Info tab in the main iTunes window, and scroll down until you see Web Browser. This is pretty easy because there's only one option here—Sync (your Web browser) Bookmarks. Turn on that checkbox, and bookmarks from your computer's Safari Web browser (on a Mac) or from Microsoft Internet Explorer (on a PC) will be copied right into your Safari Web browser on your iPod touch.

---

iTip: Deleting a Bookmark

To delete a bookmark, just tap on the Bookmarks icon, then press the Edit button in the bottom-left corner. This adds little red minus signs before each bookmark, and if you tap on one of those, a red Delete button appears on the right side of that bookmark. Tap on the red Delete button to remove that bookmark.

Completing Online Forms

If you have to enter a password to enter a website, or if you wind up buying something from a site, you're going to have to provide your name, address, payment info, etc., in an online form, and luckily Safari lets you do that in a surprisingly easy way. If it's just a text field you need to complete, then you simply tap on the field, and the keyboard appears so you can enter your info. Easy enough, but what do you do when you come across a pop-up menu (like one for the month and year your credit card expires)? When that happens, just tap on the pop-up menu and a special Safari window appears with the menu choices in a "flick wheel," where you can flick the wheel up or down with your finger until the choice you want appears with a checkmark beside it, then tap the Done button.

Using the Calculator

It's not a fancy calculator, but it's simple and the buttons and readout are quite large (it makes you feel like you're using a regular handheld calculator). To get to the Calculator, start at the Home screen and tap on Calculator. The Calculator then appears, and you use it like any other calculator—by tapping on the keys.

Finding Videos on YouTube

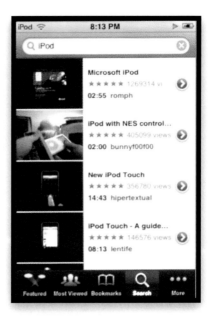

If you have Wi-Fi Internet access, you can watch videos from the online video sharing site YouTube.com, right from your iPod touch. It doesn't actually download the videos onto your iPod touch—you search for videos you want to watch, and then you watch them on your iPod touch just like would watch YouTube.com videos on your computer. However, you can bookmark your favorite videos and get right to them. Start at the Home screen and tap on YouTube. Then tap on Search (at the bottom of the screen) to bring up a search field. Tap on the search field to bring up the keyboard, type in your search term, then tap the Search button to search YouTube's vast video library. The results appear in a list below the search field. To watch one of these videos, just tap on it, then turn your iPod touch sideways (videos always play in this wide mode).

---

iTip: Getting More Video Info

To see more information about any YouTube video, tap the little blue arrow button that appears to the right of the video's name. This takes you to a screen with a detailed description of the video; there's a Bookmark button in case you want to save this video as a bookmark, and it gives you a list of related videos, as well.

Watching YouTube Videos

Once you've found a video you want to watch, just tap on it. A set of video controls will appear onscreen for pausing the video, jumping to the next video, replaying your video, and there's a slider for adjusting the volume (drag it to the right to make the video louder, to the left to make it quieter). To hide these controls, tap the screen once. To bring them back anytime, just touch the screen. To bookmark a video you like (so you can jump right to it next time), tap on the Bookmark button at the left side of the video controls. Also, at the bottom of the YouTube screen are buttons that take you directly to the featured videos of the day, YouTube's most viewed videos, your bookmarked videos, and if you tap the More button, you'll see a new set of menus that let you jump to YouTube's Most Recent videos, see their Top Rated videos, and the bottom button lets you see a History (list) of the YouTube videos you've already watched.

The Wi-Fi Version of the iTunes Store

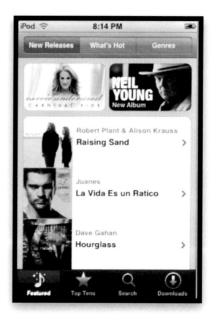

Because of its Wi-Fi capabilities, you can log into the Wi-Fi version of the iTunes Store to buy and download songs wirelessly straight from Apple right into your iPod touch, and the cool thing is: anything you buy wirelessly like this is automatically uploaded from your iPod touch to your computer the next time you sync. Here's how it works: From the Home Screen, tap on the purple iTunes button in the bottom-right corner of the screen. This takes you to a special Wi-Fi version of the iTunes Store (provided, of course, that you have an active Wi-Fi Internet connection, but you knew that, right?).

Finding Songs in the Wi-Fi iTunes Music Store

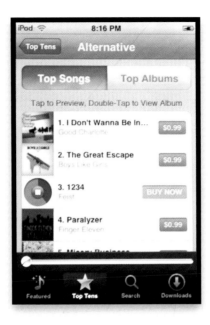

When you enter the Wi-Fi iTunes Music Store, there are four Store navigation buttons along the bottom of the screen. Tapping Featured takes you to iTunes' currently featured songs, but it also adds three new buttons to the top of the screen for direct links to New Releases, What's Hot, and a very handy listing by Genres. The second button is iTunes' Top Tens (Top 10) lists (in various categories), then the third button is Search, and tapping on it brings up a search field, and if you tap in that field, the keyboard appears so you can type in the name of the song, artist, movie, etc., you want to search the Store for. The final button, Downloads, displays the songs you've downloaded from the Wi-Fi Store. To hear a 30-second preview of any song, just tap on it. The price for each song is listed to the right of the song title, and if you tap on the price, it changes into a green Buy Now button. It will prompt you for your iTunes password (to make sure someone else isn't making buying decisions for you), and when the download starts, you can tap the Downloads button to see the download's progress. Once the song is fully downloaded, if you tap the Downloads button, the screen will be empty, but up in the top-right corner you'll see a button called Purchased and if you tap on it, you'll find it's just a shortcut to your Purchased Songs playlist, but the good news is—your down-loaded song will be in that playlist automatically.

Importing Your Calendar

Your iPod touch has a built-in calendar program and, depending on which calendar program you're using on your computer, you can import your calendar directly into your iPod touch. You can sync calendar info from either Apple's iCal or Microsoft Entourage on the Macintosh (to sync with Entourage, your calendar info must be synced with .Mac first), or if you use Windows, you can sync your calendar from Microsoft Outlook. When you connect your iPod touch to your computer for syncing, it will upload your calendar information automatically once you've turned on the Sync Calendars checkbox on the iPod Preferences Info tab. To see your imported calendar info, start at the Home screen and tap the Calendar button. You can view your calendar as one long scrolling list, or in a more traditional calendar view. To view by day, tap the Day button at the top of the screen, or tap the Month button to view the entire month (as shown here). In the Month view, if you see a small dot appearing below the date, that means you have an event scheduled for some time that day. To see the event, tap once directly on that day and that day's events will appear below the calendar. If you tap the Day view, it shows you the entire day by time, starting at 12:00 a.m. In Day view, you can navigate to other nearby dates by tapping the Left or Right Arrow buttons near the top of the screen. Anytime you want to jump to today's calendar, just tap the Today button in the top-left corner of the screen.

Importing Contacts from Your Computer

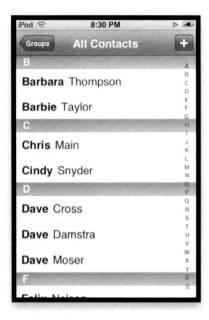

If you're a Macintosh user, there are three applications that let you sync directly from your computer to your iPod touch, and they are: (1) your Mac's Address Book application, (2) Microsoft Entourage (your Entourage Address Book must be synced with .Mac first), or (3) Yahoo! Address Book. If your contacts are in any of those three, when you sync with your computer, it launches iTunes and syncs the contacts on your computer with your iPod touch. Pretty simple stuff.

If you're a Windows user, it works pretty much the same way, but the three contact managers it supports direct importing from are: (1) Yahoo! Address Book, (2) Windows Address Book, and (3) Microsoft Outlook.

Once your contacts are in your iPod touch, to see them, start at the Home screen and tap on Contacts. This brings up a list of your contacts, and you can scroll through them using your finger on the touchscreen to flick the list upward or downward. To see the info for a contact, just tap on the name. To create a new contact, tap the + (plus sign) button in the top-right corner of the screen. This brings up a screen where you can tap on various fields, and from the keyboard that appears, type in the contact information. When you sync with your computer again, any contacts you added in your iPod touch will be copied over to your computer.

Importing Photos into Your iPod touch

Just like with an iPod classic or iPod nano, if you use Apple's iPhoto application on a Mac, or Adobe Photoshop Elements on a PC, you can have your photo albums from those applications brought over onto your iPod touch. To do that, connect your iPod touch to your computer, then in iTunes click on the Photos tab. At the top, turn on the Sync Photos From checkbox, then if you're on a Mac, choose iPhoto. (*Note:* If you don't use iPhoto, you can just put your photos into a folder, and subfolders inside that if you like, and then choose the folder of photos, instead of iPhoto.) If you're on a PC, turn on that same checkbox, but from the Sync Photos From pop-up menu, choose Adobe Photoshop Elements.

Viewing Your Imported Photos

Once you've imported photos into your iPod touch, to see them, start at the Home screen, then tap on Photos. This brings up the Photo Albums screen and at the top is Photo Library (which is a one-tap link to all the photos you've imported, all lumped together), and then a list of any separate photo albums you created, like family photos, vacation photos, etc., using Apple's iPhoto application (for Mac) or Photoshop Album or Photoshop Elements on the PC. To see thumbnails of the photos in a particular album, tap on that album. To see any photo full-screen sized, just tap on it. Once your photo is full screen, you can see other photos in that album at that size by swiping your finger on the screen in the direction you want to scroll. If your photo bounces like it's hitting a wall, you've reached the end of that album, so swipe back in the other direction. To get a better view of wide photos (photos in landscape orientation), turn your iPod touch sideways.

Viewing a Slide Show of Your Photos

Start at the Home screen, then tap on Photos to bring up the Photo Albums screen. To see any photo album as a slide show, just tap on the album, then when the thumbnails appear, at the bottom of the window is a Play button. Tap on it to start the slide show. To stop your slide show, just tap the screen once, then tap the name of your album that appears in the top-left corner of the screen. The iPod touch slide shows come complete with smooth built-in dissolve transitions between each photo, but if you want to choose a different type of dissolve, or change the length of time each photo appears onscreen, then start at the Home screen and tap on Settings. When the Settings screen appears, tap on Photos, which brings up a list of options for your slide show. To change any setting, just tap on it. You can also turn on Repeat to loop your slide show, or Shuffle to play your slides in a random order. When you're done, tap the Settings button in the upper-left corner.

Adding Background Music to Your Slide Show

PHOTO BY SCOTT KELBY

There really isn't a slide show feature that lets you include music (at least at this point), so we're going to do a workaround (it's a little clunky, but it works). Start at the Home screen, and then tap on the orange Music button. In the Music screen, tap on Songs at the bottom, and scroll to the song you want as background music for your slide show. Tap on the song and the music starts playing. Now, press the Home button to return to the Home screen, tap on the Photos button, then tap on the album you want to see as a slide show. Tap the Play button that appears at the bottom of the album's thumbnails screen, and there you have it—your slide show playing with background music playing behind it.

---

iTip: Changing Photos' Order

To change the order of your photos, you have to go back to your computer, change the order the photos appear in the album on your computer, then go to iTunes and sync your iPod touch with your computer, and it will update your iPod with the new order.

Make a Photo Your Startup Wallpaper

Each time your wake your iPod touch from sleep (and believe me, it will be asleep a lot), you're greeted with an unlock screen. By default, this unlock screen uses a NASA photo of the earth taken from space. (I guess I didn't really have to mention that it was taken from space. I mean, where else could a photo of the entire earth be taken from?) However, you can choose any one of your photos for this wake-up background wallpaper instead. To do that, start at the Home screen, tap on Photos, then tap on Photo Library and scroll through your photos until you find the one you want to use as your wallpaper. Tap on it to see it full screen. Now, tap once on the little icon in the bottom-left corner, and a button appears on the lower right for Set Wallpaper. Tap that button, and that photo becomes your new "wake-up" wallpaper.

---

iTip: Pinch to Zoom

To get a closer look at any photo, just tap on the photo to see it full screen, then pinch two fingers together in the center of the screen and spread them outward to zoom in. To zoom in tighter, pinch outward once again. To return to the normal-size view, just double-tap on the screen.

Chapter Nine

Home Sweet Home

iTunes Essentials

▶▶ Now, I know what you're thinking: "How does Motley Crue's 'Home Sweet Home' tie into a chapter about the basic, most essential things you need to know about iTunes?" First, many of you will be using iTunes at home. (Unless of course, you're like my employees, who use iTunes all day long in lieu of working productively. In fact, when I'm roaming the halls, I'm not sure which I see more on their monitors—iTunes, eBay, Amazon .com, or CNN. Once I even saw someone with Photoshop open, but thankfully it was just because they were color-correcting an album cover they were going to use in iTunes. Whew—that was a close one!) Anyway, since some of you will be using iTunes at home, especially when you first get your iPod, I thought there was some loose thread I could use to connect your using your iPod there with the word "home" in "Home Sweet Home." Hey, it's fairly "loose" I know, but my backup plan was to use the song "Essential" by The Gravy, from their album "Lollipolyp." I didn't have a problem with the "polyp" part of it (as icky as that is), but if the chapter title was "Essential" and the subtitle was "iTunes Essentials," you'd think I took the easy way out, and you deserve more than that. You deserve a title that is so loosely related to the actual topic of the chapter that it takes more than 300 words to explain why I chose it. See, just when you think you've got me figured out, I zig when you thought I'd zag (I have no idea what that means). Quick, turn the page before I think of something else to write here.

Limiting How Much iTunes Displays

In the iTunes main window (where you see your songs), there are separate columns that display the song title, the artist, the album name, and a host of other information. Some of it you probably will care about (like the song name, artist, time, etc.), and some of it you probably won't need to see. Ever. Stuff like a song's Beats Per Minute (although this column is helpful to DJs). Luckily, you can customize your columns and choose which ones are visible (and which ones are hidden), which makes for very clean, easy-to-read playlists, because they display just the info you care about seeing. Here's how to customize yours: Press Command-J (PC: Ctrl-J) on your keyboard to bring up the iTunes View Options dialog. Select which columns you'd like to be visible by turning on (or off) the checkboxes next to the column names. When you're done, click OK and only the checked columns will appear in your main window.

---

iTip: Making Hidden Columns Visible

If at any time you decide you want a hidden column to be visible, just Control-click (PC: Right-click) directly on one of the column headers. This brings up a contextual menu of column choices. Just choose the column you want to see (hidden ones will be the ones without a checkmark), and that column will now be visible. To hide any column, you do the same trick, but uncheck the column you wish to hide.

Getting More Song Info

iTunes' status display (that rectangular panel at the top center of the iTunes window) shows you the name of the current song, the artist, how much of the song has already played (the elapsed time)—in minutes and seconds, as well as in a progress bar—and how much time is left until the song has finished playing (the remaining time). If you'd like the name of the album the song came from, click directly on the artist's name (the artist's name and the album name scroll continuously under the static song name). Want the total time of the song? Click on the Remaining Time (on the right side of the progress bar).

---

iTip: Skipping a Song

To the left of each song title is a checkbox, and every checked song will play when playing an entire playlist. If you want to skip a song, just uncheck its checkbox. This also works when importing songs from an audio CD—checked songs are imported, unchecked songs are not.

Editing Your Song's Info

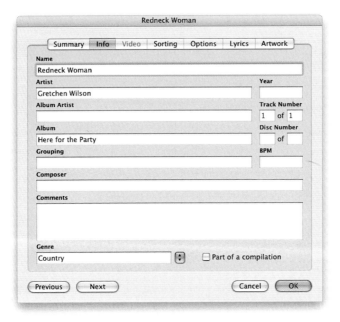

If you want to change, update, or add any information to a song, just Control-click (PC: Right-click) on the song, and from the contextual menu that appears, choose Get Info. When the dialog appears, click on the Info tab and you'll see a number of fields where you can edit or add information about the song. This is the same information that will appear in the status display (in the top center of the iTunes window) when a song is playing, but you can also include additional information, like the year it was recorded, your own personal comments, and the song's composer. When you're done, just click the OK button.

---

iTip: Playing a Song

There are really four different ways to play a song within iTunes, so you should try them all to find out which one best suits your personal style. Here they are: (1) find the song you want to play and just double-click on it; (2) click on the song you want to play and then press the Spacebar on your keyboard; (3) click on the song you want to hear, then click on the Play button in the upper left-hand corner of the iTunes window; or (4) click on the song you want to play and choose Play from the Controls menu.

Editing More Than One Song at One Time

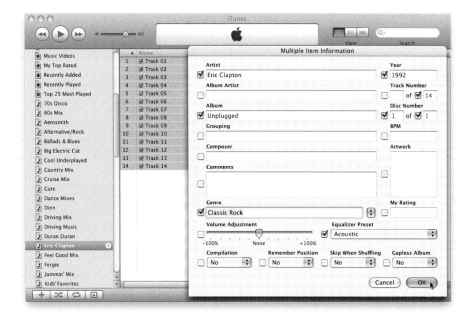

You know by now how to edit a song's info (using the Get Info dialog), but what if you want to edit a bunch of songs at once (for example, let's say you imported 14 songs from an album, and you want to add the album name to each of the 14 songs)? You do that by Command-clicking (PC: Ctrl-clicking) on the songs you want to edit (in this case, all 14 songs you just imported), and then Control-clicking (PC: Right-clicking) on any one of those 14 songs, and choosing Get Info. Rather than the standard Get Info dialog, a Multiple Item Information dialog will appear instead. (Well, the first time you do this, you'll get a warning dialog that says: "Are you sure you want to edit information for multiple items?" Just click Yes.) Now the information you enter in this dialog will be applied to all the selected songs. When you're done, just click OK.

Updating Just One Info Field

If you want to change just one bit of info on a song (for example, let's say you had the song "And the Cradle Will Rock" by Van Halen listed as coming from their album *Diver Down* when everyone who's anyone knows that song actually came from the album *Women and Children First*), here's good news: you don't have to bring up the whole Get Info dialog for just this one little change. Instead, just click on the song, and then click once directly on the album's current name to highlight the Album field. Now, just type in the new name over the old name, then press the Return (PC: Enter) key to lock in your change. It probably goes without saying, but I'm going to say it anyway—this also works for editing other fields, like Name, Artist, etc.

Adding Your Own Custom Genres

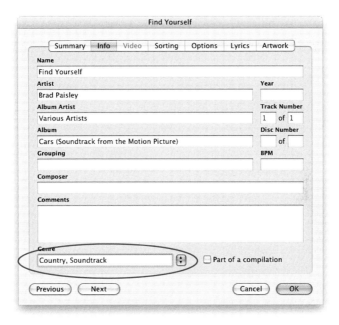

Although iTunes comes with a preset list of popular genres, there are some it just doesn't include (like Salsa, Thrash, or New Wave), and you can probably come up with a dozen or so yourself. That's why iTunes lets you create your own custom genres (like Death Metal or Opera). To create your own custom genre, Control-click (PC: Right-click) on any song, and then choose Get Info from the contextual menu that appears. When the Get Info dialog appears, click on the Info tab, and then just type the name you want for your "new" genre in the Genre field (how about Broadway Musicals or Gospel?) and click OK. If you want to create a genre that encompasses a number of different styles, just put a comma after each name (like Metal, Jazz, Punk, Choral). Assigning these "multiple genres" to a song will cause the song to appear in multiple categories when searching or browsing. For example, you might want the Brad Paisley song "Find Yourself" to have multiple genres, so it appears when you search for either Country or Soundtrack (it was part of the soundtrack for the movie *Cars*). When browsing, it would appear in a new genre labeled "Country, Soundtrack."

Help for People Who Don't Know the Words

If you have an iPod nano (or any newer iPod), and you're really bad at remembering the words to songs, then "hang on—help is on its way" (sorry about that lame Little River Band reference). Here's the deal: in iTunes 5, Apple added the ability to embed lyrics into your songs (just like you embed the genre, the rating, album art, etc.) and best of all, these lyrics can be viewed on your iPod nano or newer iPod. Here's how to set it up: In iTunes, select the song you want to add lyrics for, go under the File menu and choose Get Info. When the Get Info dialog appears, click on the Lyrics tab, and type in the words. Simple enough. Now, if you don't know the words, you can fire up your Web browser, then go to one of the many (and by many, I mean about a-bazillion) lyrics websites. (By the way, the Lyrics field in iTunes supports copying-and-pasting. I'm just sayin'.) Now, once a song is playing on your iPod nano, you can view these lyrics by just pressing the center Select button a few times until the lyrics appear onscreen.

---

iTip: Formats without Lyrics

As luck would have it, there are two file formats that you can't add lyrics to: QuickTime files and WAV files. So, what do you do? Convert it to a format that does support lyrics. Click on the file, go under the iTunes Advanced menu, and choose Convert Selection to AAC (or Convert Selection to MP3, or whatever your preference setting is set to). Bam. That's it.

Changing the Sort Order: Last to First

By default, iTunes columns are sorted in either alphabetical order or numerically (from the lowest number to the highest). You can determine how iTunes is sorting by looking for the column that has the little arrow in its right-hand corner. If the arrow is facing upward, the column is sorted from A to Z (alphabetically) or from lowest number to highest (numerically). However, if you'd prefer to have it sort backwards (so you'd hear Sheryl Crow's "Real Gone" before you'd hear "Ain't No Other Man" by Christina Aguilera), just click once on the Artist column header. This reverses the alphabetical order (you'll now see the little arrow in the Artist column pointing downward), putting "Real Gone" at the top of the playlist (or if you click on a numerical column, like Time, then your longest song would be first, followed by your next longest, etc., until your shortest song appeared at the bottom). Also, if you click on the Rating column, your 5-star songs will appear at the top of the iTunes window, and if you click again, they'll appear at the bottom of the iTunes window.

Finding the Song That's Playing Now

When you play a song, a tiny speaker icon appears to the right of the track number to let you know that song is playing. However, while that song is playing you can go and do other things (like sorting another playlist, changing song names, etc.). So, although you may be playing the song "Let's Get Loud" by Jennifer Lopez, that song won't be highlighted because you're working in an entirely different playlist. Then, how do you find the song that's currently playing? Just press Command-L (PC: Ctrl-L), which instantly jumps you to the song that's currently playing, even if it's in a different playlist.

---

iTip: Repeating Your Music

If you can't get enough of a particular song (or a particular playlist for that matter), you can have iTunes automatically repeat it by clicking on the Repeat Playlist/Song button (it's the third button from the left in the bottom-left corner of the iTunes window). If you click once on this button, iTunes will repeat your entire current playlist. Click again and it will replay the current song over and over and over again (toddlers love this feature). To stop the repeating, click the button again.

Use Browsing to Create Instant Playlists

Let's say you want to hear nothing but country songs today, but you don't have a Country playlist. Or maybe you just want to hear all your Aerosmith songs but didn't make an Aerosmith playlist either. Then you should try iTunes' Browse feature, which lets you (in just a couple of clicks) have a playlist of your favorite artist, or genre, or album. Here's how: In the Library section on the left side of iTunes, click on Music, then click on the Browse button in the bottom-right corner of the iTunes window (it's shown circled above in red). This gives you three main categories to browse by: Genre, Artist, and Album. In the Genre list click on Country and all your Country songs will instantly appear (well, at least all the songs you tagged with Country as the genre). Just double-click the first song in the list and it begins playing that list. It's that fast and easy. (*Note:* To turn off the Browse feature, click on that Eye icon again.)

---

iTip: Changing Browse Categories

Some people just don't like taking the time to add genres to all their songs, so if you're not a "genre" person, you may as well hide the Genre category when you're browsing. Just go to the iTunes Preferences (on a Mac, it's under the iTunes menu; on a Windows PC, it's under the Edit menu) and click on the General icon. Then turn off the checkbox for Show Genre When Browsing.

Finding a Song

Once you have a couple hundred (or more) songs in your Music Library, finding one particular song can start to become time-consuming. When you have a few thousand, it's needle-in-the-haystack time. That's why iTunes has a Search field in the upper right-hand corner of the iTunes window (it's the field with the Magnifying Glass icon in it). While in the Music Library, just begin typing the name of the song, album, or artist, and as you start typing, iTunes will immediately start searching. As soon as it finds a match (even if you haven't finished typing), it'll display the matches in the main window. To clear the search results and return to the full playlist, just click on the little gray circle with an X in it (on the right side of the Search field). One more thing: if you click on the Music Library before you start your search, it searches all the music you have in iTunes. If you want to search within just a particular playlist, click on that playlist first, then start your search—now it only searches in that particular playlist.

Searching Made Smarter

Let's say that you want to find the song "Cars" by Gary Numan, so you type "car" up in the Search field (makes sense, right?). In the iTunes on my computer, this brings up 27 results—everything from the song "Car Wash" to songs from the *Cars* soundtrack, because it brings up any song in your Music Library that contains the word "car," from the song "Carolina in My Mind" to the band Yellowcard. But you can narrow your search right off the bat by using the Search pop-up menu (which is actually that little Magnifying Glass icon—it's more than just an icon, it's a pop-up menu). So, click-and-hold on that little Magnifying Glass icon, and from the pop-up menu that appears, choose Song. Now it only searches the names of songs in your Music Library, and not the album or artist. This greatly narrows your search, and gets you to the the songs you want much faster. By the way, when you're done searching, just press the gray X in the right side of the Search field.

Clearing a Song's Play Count

As you may know by now, iTunes keeps a count of each time you play a particular song, but if at any time you'd like to wipe that play count clean (for example, if you're having friends over and you don't want them to see that you've played "Lover Girl" by Teena Marie 87 times), just Control-click (PC: Right-click) on the song and from the contextual menu that appears, choose Reset Play Count. iTunes will reset your play count to zero. Your secret will now be safe forever, and your friends will think you're cool once again. (*Note:* Although you've cleared the Play Count field, the Last Played field will still show—obviously—the last time you played the song, so there's still a chance that might give your secret away....)

Deleting Songs

If you've had enough of a song and you just want it out of iTunes (and out of your life), just click on the song and press the Delete (PC: Backspace) key on your keyboard. You can also delete a song by Control-clicking (PC: Right-clicking) on a song and choosing Delete from the contextual menu. From the first dialog that appears, choose Remove, then choose Move to Trash (PC: Recycle Bin) from the next dialog. If the song is in a playlist, iTunes will remove the song from just that playlist. If you click on a song in your Music Library, then iTunes removes the file altogether and puts it in the Trash (on a Mac) or the Recycle Bin (on a PC). Don't freak out—you'll get a warning dialog before it does either, so you don't have to worry about hitting the wrong key and losing a beloved treasured favorite, like "White Wedding" by Billy Idol.

---

iTip: Deleting Multiple Songs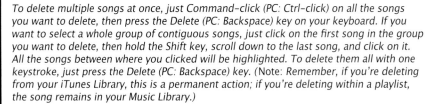

To delete multiple songs at once, just Command–click (PC: Ctrl–click) on all the songs you want to delete, then press the Delete (PC: Backspace) key on your keyboard. If you want to select a whole group of contiguous songs, just click on the first song in the group you want to delete, then hold the Shift key, scroll down to the last song, and click on it. All the songs between where you clicked will be highlighted. To delete them all with one keystroke, just press the Delete (PC: Backspace) key. (Note: Remember, if you're deleting from your iTunes Library, this is a permanent action; if you're deleting within a playlist, the song remains in your Music Library.)

---

iTunes' Built-In VU Meters

If you ever need to see a graphic display of the audio frequencies in your song (it's helpful when you're recording so you don't record at too high a volume, which causes distortion), go up to the status display (in the top center of the iTunes window) and on the far-left side of the display, click on the dark-gray circular button with the right-facing arrow. When you do this, two digital VU (volume unit) meters will appear where the song info usually appears, giving you a visualization of the music frequencies (just in case you care). Click on that arrow button again to bring back the song title.

Organizing the Songs on Your Hard Disk

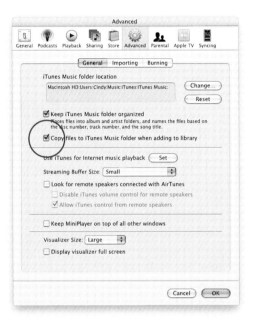

If you have an MP3 song on your hard disk and you double-click on it, iTunes opens it and plays the song. It also creates an invisible shortcut (or alias) to that song from that folder on your hard disk. There's nothing wrong with this, but what you'll eventually have are folders scattered all over your hard disk with music in them. Well, you can make things much more organized than that (which makes backing up your music much easier) by having iTunes copy each song that it plays into the iTunes Music folder. That way, all of your music is in one place. To turn on this feature, go to the iTunes Preferences (on a Mac, it's under the iTunes menu; on a Windows PC, it's under the Edit menu), and click on the Advanced icon. In the Advanced section, click on the General tab and turn on the checkbox for Copy Files to iTunes Music Folder When Adding to Library. Now you can click OK, with the peace of mind that can only come from bringing order and harmony to your music world.

---

iTip: Consolidating Your Music

If you've already got music scattered all over your hard disk, it's not too late—you can have iTunes go to all those folders and copy all the songs listed in your Music Library into the iTunes Music folder on your hard disk in just one click. Go under the Advanced menu and choose Consolidate Library. It wouldn't hurt if you played the song "Come Together" by The Beatles while you're doing this.

Straight from CD to Playlist

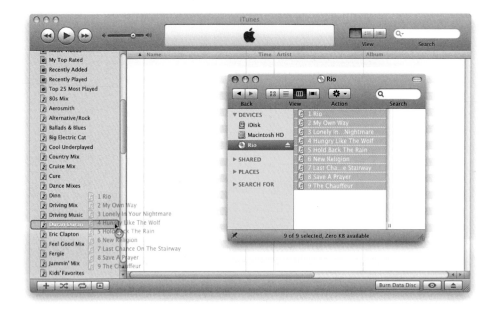

When you import songs from a CD, it usually works like this: you import the songs; you find them in your iTunes Library; and then you drag these imported songs into a playlist. Want to skip a step? When you import a CD, select the songs on the CD (by Shift-clicking on the first and last song in the CD's folder on your hard disk), and drag them right into that new playlist. When they import, of course, they'll be in your Music Library, but they'll also be in your desired playlist. Hey, if it saves time, I'm all for it.

---

iTip: Adding MP3 Songs

If you have MP3 songs already on your hard disk that you want to add to your iTunes Music Library, it's easy: Just go under the File menu and choose Add to Library. This brings up a standard Open dialog, so you can navigate to where the songs are on your hard disk, then click the Choose button to add them. Of course, there's an even easier way—just open the folder that has your MP3 songs, drag-and-drop them right into iTunes, and they'll be imported. It doesn't get much easier than that.

Set Up Your CDs to Import Automatically

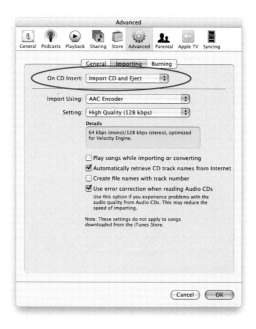

If you've decided to import your entire collection of CDs into iTunes (and I whole-heartedly recommend that), then you're going to want to have as much automation as possible, so you don't go totally brain-dead during the process. Here's why: When you insert a CD, it doesn't import the tracks. Instead, it just shows you what's on the CD, which is great if you only want to hear what's on the CD. But if you're cataloguing your entire collection, this is the last thing you want it to do. Instead, imagine how much time it would save if you just inserted a CD and iTunes automatically imported all the songs, then spit the CD out, ready for you to insert the next disc? It can do just that—you just have to tell it to. Go to the iTunes Preferences (found under the iTunes menu on a Mac; the Edit menu on a Windows PC), click on the Advanced icon, and then click on the Importing tab. From the On CD Insert pop-up menu, choose Import CD and Eject, and then click OK. That's it—you just turned your computer into an automatic CD-importing machine, which enables you to pay your little brother to sit there and swap the ejected CDs for a few hours while you go to a concert. See, this is what life's all about.

Auto-Naming for Imported CD Songs

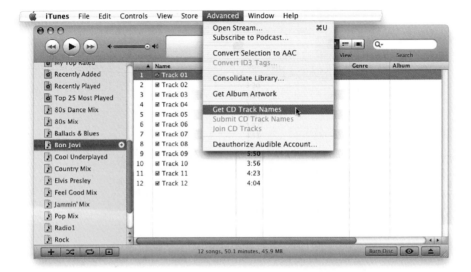

If you're importing songs from a CD, and you have a continuous Internet connection, iTunes automatically finds the names (and other background info) for all the songs you're importing. Here's what actually happens: When you import, iTunes will go to the Web and search within the massive Gracenote CDDB Internet Audio Database for the info on the CD you're importing. If it finds the information, iTunes will automatically download that information into each song's info panel, naming the songs (artists, album names, etc.) as it goes (pretty cool, eh?). If you don't have a continuous Internet connection, just add all of your songs to your iTunes Music Library or playlists, connect to the Internet, then under the Advanced menu, choose Get CD Track Names.

Save Hard Disk Space When Importing CDs

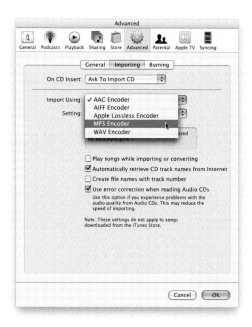

When you import music from CDs, by default iTunes converts your songs into AAC format (which is great in that it compresses the size of your song files while maintaining CD-quality sound). But if you need to import smaller-sized files (and you don't mind a decrease in sound quality), you can choose to import songs as MP3s. Just go into iTunes' Preferences (under the iTunes menu on a Mac; the Edit menu on a Windows PC), click on the Advanced icon, and then click on the Importing tab. From the Import Using pop-up menu, choose MP3 Encoder (or any other file format you'd like). Now when you import CD songs, they'll be in the format you want. (By the way, all songs from the regular iTunes Store are protected AAC encoded, meaning the file can't be "shared," while most CD-imported files are unprotected AAC encoded, meaning the files can be shared.)

Combining Two Tracks into One

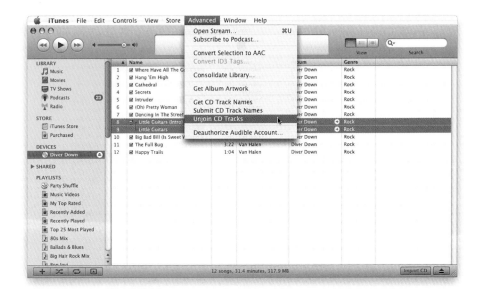

Sometimes when you import a song from a CD, if the song has a lengthy introduction, it can get separated from the song. For example, look at Van Halen's "Little Guitars." It starts with a legendary guitar solo from Eddie Van Halen that actually has its own name ("Little Guitars [Intro]"), but if you hear this song on classic rock radio stations, the two are played as one song, the intro goes right into the song. It's really one song, and when you import it from the CD, there's a decent chance iTunes will import it as one song, but if iTunes thinks these are two separate songs, there will be a gap of a few seconds between songs. If that happens, no sweat—just Command-click (PC: Ctrl-click) on the two songs before they're imported and then go under the Advanced menu and choose Join CD Tracks. Now, they'll import as one song, with no gap in between (you'll know that they're linked because a tiny bracket icon will appear next to the two songs' names). By the way, if you ever want to really mess with rock history, you can select both songs, go under the Advanced menu, and choose Unjoin CD Tracks. (*Note:* This whole joining thing can only happen *before* the CD tracks are imported into iTunes—not after.)

Salvaging Damaged CDs

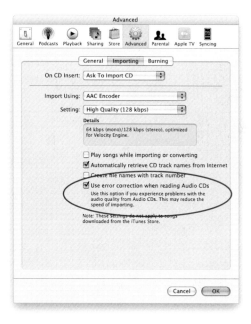

If you find out that your little sister has been using one of your prized CDs as a Frisbee, you're probably going to find that out when you play the CD in iTunes. It's going to have its share of scratches, junk, and other nasty stuff, which makes importing these tracks nearly out of the question—unless you know about this somewhat weird and obscure preference setting. To find it, go into the iTunes Preferences (found under the iTunes menu on a Mac; the Edit menu on a Windows PC), click on the Advanced icon, and then click on the Importing tab. Now turn on the checkbox for Use Error Correction When Reading Audio CDs. iTunes will then do its darnedest to correct a disc's trauma while importing, salvaging as much as it can. It doesn't work 100% of the time, but when it does, it's worth its weight in Starbucks coffee.

Burning a CD

Burning a CD is a breeze, but there are a couple of things you should know before you do it, just so it's even breezier (if that's even a word). First, you can only burn playlists (not your Music Library), so click on a playlist in the Source list that you want to burn (also, don't insert a blank CD yet—wait until it asks you to). So now that you've selected a playlist, take a quick look down at the bottom center of the iTunes window to make sure you don't have more than 1.2 hours of music in your playlist (that's pretty much the amount of time you can fit onto an audio CD these days). If you have too many songs, delete some songs until you have less than 1.2 hours. Then click on the Burn Disc button (it's in the bottom right-hand corner of the iTunes window). The top-center status display will prompt you: Please Insert a Blank Disc (that's your cue). Once you insert a blank CD, iTunes will begin burning the songs in your playlist onto your blank CD. (*Note:* Now's your chance to abort burning the CD, if you so desire, by clicking on the X in the status display, although the formerly blank CD will no longer be usable.) Assuming all goes well, iTunes will spit your new music CD out of your CD drive.

---

iTip: Skipping Songs in a Playlist

If there's a song in your playlist that you don't want to appear on a CD that you're getting ready to burn, just click on the checkbox that appears right before the song's name to deselect it, and when the CD burns, iTunes will skip over the unchecked song.

Fitting More Songs on Your CDs

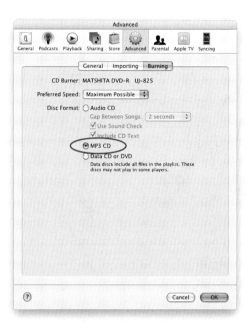

If you want to fit the maximum number of songs on your CDs, you might want to try burning an MP3 CD rather than an audio CD (provided of course that your CD player can read MP3 CDs—many new CD players can, but not all). Because the MP3 format uses a high rate of compression, you'll be able to fit many more songs on a CD in MP3 format, but to do that, you'll need to change an iTunes Preferences setting. So, go to iTunes Preferences (found under the iTunes menu on a Mac; the Edit menu on a Windows PC), click on the Advanced icon, and then click on the Burning tab. Under the Disc Format section, click on MP3 CD, and then click OK. That's all there is to it—now you just have to hope that your CD player supports MP3 CDs. (*Note:* This doesn't work for iTunes Store songs or songs in AAC format.)

Setting the Gap Between Burned Songs

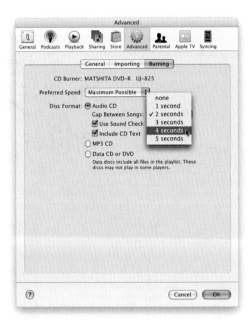

So your CDs don't sound like one long, unending song, iTunes adds a 2-second pause (or gap) between songs by default. Besides being sorely needed from a listening perspective, the gap also helps your CD player recognize individual tracks. Although 2 seconds is the default setting, you can change the length of the gap so it's longer, shorter, or you can eliminate the gap altogether (which you might want to do if you're listening to an audiobook or the recording of a speech). To do that, go to the iTunes Preferences (found under the iTunes menu on a Mac; the Edit menu on a Windows PC), click on the Advanced icon, and then click on the Burning tab. Choose your desired length (in seconds) from the Gap Between Songs pop-up menu, and then click OK. That length now becomes the gap setting for your burned CDs.

Want to Find a Spot in a Song? Live Scrub It!

Another helpful thing Apple added in iTunes 7 was the ability to "live scrub" through a song. This may not sound like a big deal, until you realize how it was done before. For example, let's take the song "Bawitdaba" by Kid Rock. It has this crazy long intro thing with weird sounds, and well…I just want to get to the song. Before iTunes 7, you could grab the scrubber bar at the top of the iTunes window and drag it to the right to jump past that part, but while you dragged it was totally silent, so when you let go of the scrubber bar, you were just guessing if you were in the right spot or not. So, it was kind of a hit-or-miss proposition. But in iTunes 7, Apple changed that scrubber bar to be live, so you can hear the music (in fast-forward speed) as you scrub. You can hear when the annoying (I mean, "inspired") intro is finished, so you can stop right where that 1-minute-plus long intro ends. Ahhhhh, that's better. (Come on, everybody sing with me, "Bawitdaba da bang da dang diggy diggy, diggy said the boogy said up jump the boogy!").

Play Live Albums without Gaps

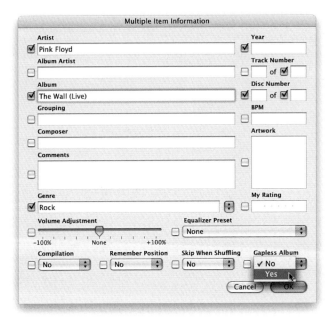

At last, you can set up iTunes so live albums played in iTunes, or on your iPod, will play as one performance—without the gaps (short pauses) between songs that have been a part of every previous version of iTunes. But it's not just for live albums, it's also for classical albums, and Pink Floyd albums, and Brian Wilson's "Smile," which will finally sound like one contiguous thing!!!!! What a glorious day this is in our otherwise featureless and banal lives (sorry, I got carried away). Anyway, this is called "gapless playback" and here's how to invoke its majestic power and authoritative dominion (sorry—again—carried away). In iTunes, select all the songs that you want to have this gapless playback (so, for example, you'd hold the Command key on a Mac [or the Ctrl key on a PC] and click on all the songs from a live album or classical album), then press Command-I (PC: Ctrl-I) to bring up the Multiple Item Information dialog (this lets you change the settings for a number of songs at once, and this only appears when you've first selected more than one song). In the bottom-right corner of the dialog, you'll see a pop-up menu for Gapless Album. Just choose Yes from the pop-up menu, and then click OK. That's it—the gaps are gone.

How Much Room Is Left for Videos?

Want to know how much room you have left on your iPod for music and video podcasts, and photos, etc., while it's connected to your computer? Then just click on it in the iTunes Source list and you'll be taken to the iPod Preferences Summary window that not only displays a large icon of your iPod, but it gives you all the inside info on your iPod, including how much space is available, and how much of that space is taken up by music, videos, and photos, via a bar graph at the bottom of the window. That way, you know at a glance right where you stand.

---

iTip: Personalized Color

Want an idea of how smart the Preferences window is? Take a look at the drawing of your iPod. Did you notice the drawing matches the color of your iPod? That's right, if you've got a red iPod nano, a drawing of a red iPod nano is what you see in the Preferences Summary window. They could have put a generic iPod drawing there, but putting a drawing of the same exact color that you own is a totally Apple thing to do. Just another reason why the iPod is what it is.

Hiding the MiniStore

The iTunes MiniStore (that convenience store version of the full iTunes Store that appears at the bottom of your main window) can be turned off (it's on by default) fairly easily—you just have to know where to look. Just go under the View menu (in the menu bar at the top) and choose Hide MiniStore (or use the keyboard shortcut Command-Shift-M on a Mac, or Ctrl-Shift-M on a PC).

---

iTip: Single-Letter Shortcut

Another little-known tip: you can jump to playlists in the Source list by simply typing the first letter of the playlist you want to jump to. If you don't have a playlist with a particular letter, it will jump to any existing item in the Source list. For example, if you don't have a playlist that starts with the letter P, if you press P on your keyboard it will jump to Party Shuffle. Note: This one-key shortcut works as long as any item is highlighted in the Source list.

Chapter Ten

Proof of Purchase
Using the iTunes Store

Apple changed the music industry forever when it introduced the iTunes Store with its "fair play" technology, which preserves the rights of the artists who make their music available for legal download. It was revolutionary, and more importantly, it worked. Now more than six million songs are available for legal download from the iTunes Store. I sometimes call it the ITS for short, because writing out "iTunes Store" each time gets really old really fast. Not just for me, mind you, but for you—the reader. That's why acronyms exist. People get tired of reading, writing, and even saying long names. For example, my full legal name (as it appears on my birth certificate) is: Stephen Charles Oscar Theodore Thaddeus Kevin Edward Lawrence Bradley Young. After painstakingly writing it out that way for more than 26 years, I finally came up with the acronym SCOTT KELBY instead, which is much easier to write, and best of all, its meaning is pretty obvious to your average person (kind of like IBM or UPS). For the next three years, I always wrote the acronym in all caps, but once I realized that most people knew what it stood for (like ASAP or NFL), I then dropped the cap on everything but the first letter of each word, making it just Scott Kelby. Now, about the name of this chapter—it's actually a band's name, Proof of Purchase, and (as of the writing of this book) you can find two of their songs on the ITS. I listened to the 30-second preview of their song "Fallacy," and it scared the livin' crap out of me. Don't ever listen to that preview with the light outs. It's way too Eerie, Creepy, and Scary. It's ECS.

Making Your Way Around the iTunes Store

You can visit the iTunes store by clicking on iTunes Store (under the Store listing on the left side of the iTunes window, shown circled here in red). The iTunes Store is a lot like a website, in that there's a homepage, and then you click links to visit other pages (in fact, you can't access the iTunes Store unless you have an Internet connection, so it's kind of like iTunes is a Web browser for the store). There are three columns in the homepage, and you access the main areas of the Store (Music, Movies, TV Shows, etc.) by clicking on the links at the top of the left column. You can always get back to this homepage by clicking on the little Home button that appears near the top-left corner of the iTunes main window. If you want to navigate back to the previous page, just press the Back button (to the left of the Home button). In fact, if you ever get lost, you'll see little tabs that show the path that got you where you currently are. These little tabs are clickable, so you can use those to get back to a previous screen.

---

iTip: Navigation Keyboard Shortcuts

Just like a Web browser, you can return to your previous page by using keyboard short-cuts. For example, to jump back one page, press Command-[(PC: Ctrl-[). That's the Left Bracket key—it's immediately to the right of the letter P on your keyboard. To jump forward one page, press Command-] (PC: Ctrl-])—that's the Right Bracket key.

The Homepage Navigation Dots

In the center column of the iTunes Store homepage there are special areas for new releases and iTunes Store exclusives, what's hot, staff favorites, freebies, and indies. Although only a few titles are currently visible, there are actually more. To see the other titles, just click the blue circular arrow buttons that appear on the left and right side of each area (they're circled above). So, how many times do you need to click to see everything? Here's how to tell: In the title bar of each of these areas are little round navigation dots. If you see three dots, there are three screens of info. You can also click on any dot to jump directly to a panel of titles (so if you wanted to jump to the third set, you'd click on the third little circle). To get back to the original homepage set, click on the first circle again. See, it's the little things, isn't it?

---

iTip: Seeing All New Releases

Want to take a quick look at what's been added to the iTunes Store recently? Of course, you could scroll through the featured New Releases section or navigate using the little dots at the top of the New Releases box. But if you use this shortcut, you'll be able to see what's new this week, last week, the week before that, and the week before that. That's right, instead of clicking on the left or right blue arrows, just click right on the words "See All" in the upper right-hand corner of the New Releases box. A page will appear that lists everything that's been new for the last four weeks. Nice.

You Can Browse in the iTunes Store Too!

Genre browsing really works well in the iTunes Store because Apple assigned a genre to every song in the Store. So, if you want to browse through all the Comedy tracks, just click on the Browse button in the bottom-right corner, and in the iTunes Store list on the left, click on Music, then click on Comedy in the Genre list, and then in the Subgenre list, click on All. All the comedians that have downloadable tracks will then appear in the Artist list (in the top center), and if you click on an artist, all of his or her albums appear along the top-right side. Click on an album, and those tracks will appear in the main window. *Warning:* If you try this a few times in the iTunes Store, you'll most likely love it, and then you'll start using genre browsing in your own Library, even though you thought you didn't like browsing. Hey, I'm just sayin'.

---

iTip: Almost Everything Is Clickable

There's more to the iTunes Store than meets the eye, because almost everything you see is a clickable link. So if you do a search and some album covers appear at the top of the window, try moving your cursor over the text beside an album—like over the artist's name. It'll highlight with a link that'll take you not just to the album, but to all that artist's work. By the way, you can even click on the Explicit warning text, and you'll get a detailed description of just what "explicit" means. Just in case you were wondering, it means "really naughty stuff."

Making Your Searches Make Sense

When you get the results of a search, they're listed in order of their relevance to the song name (or artist, etc.) you entered. However, that doesn't mean the song you want is on top—quite the contrary—so I usually wind up re-sorting these results by something else to help find the song I'm looking for. For example, I'm searching for the song "The Other Side" (the Aerosmith version), but when I type "Other Side" in the Search field, there are 150 results, and the one at the top of the list (sorted by Relevance) is "Otherside" by Red Hot Chili Peppers. So what's the quickest way for me to find the Aerosmith version? Click on the Artist column, which re-sorts these results alphabetically by author, sending Red Hot Chili Peppers toward the bottom of the list, and Aerosmith closer to the top (since it sorts by the first name, I just have to scroll through the A's, but it'll still be faster and easier to find them).

---

iTip: Speeding Through Previews

Since there are more than six million songs in the iTunes Store, you can bet there are multiple versions of certain songs (even multiple versions by the same artist—the live version, the unplugged version, etc.), and finding the right version of your song may take listening to a lot of 30-second previews. However, you can speed things up by using this trick: once the list of matching songs appears, double-click the first song in the list, and the moment you realize that it's not the version you want, just hit the Right Arrow key on your keyboard and the next version's preview will play. Keep hittin' that Right Arrow until you find the right version. This is one huge timesaving shortcut!

Can't Find It? Try a Power Search!

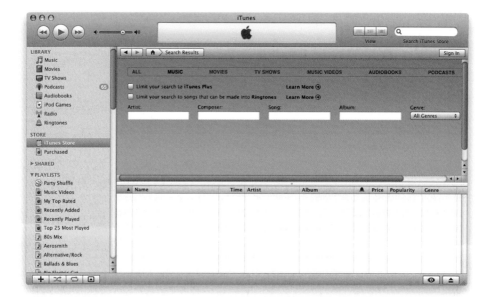

If the regular iTunes Store Search doesn't do the trick for you (maybe you're looking for some really obscure song and just aren't finding it, but you figure it's probably there somewhere—maybe you don't have the correct spelling of the artist's name, or something like that), you can try a Power Search, which lets you really refine your criteria. To do a Power Search, go to the iTunes Store homepage and click Power Search under Quick Links on the top-right side of the screen. A more detailed search area will appear across the top of your main window. Now you can search in multiple areas (like searching by Artist, Composer, Song, Album, and/or Genre) all at once. Hey, it's worth a try.

---

iTip: Apple's Music Request Form

If you've searched the iTunes Store and the song you want just isn't available yet, what can you do? Tell Apple. That's right, Apple has a music request form so you can tell them which songs you'd like to see added to the iTunes Store. To find this online form, visit www.apple.com/feedback/itunes.html and when you get there, in the Comments field tell them the name of the song(s) and the artist(s) you'd like to see added. It's no guarantee, but if you want it badly enough to let Apple know, you're probably not alone, and the more times they hear it, the better chance you'll soon find it on the ITS. Give it a shot.

Finding Songs from When You Graduated

Remember all those great songs from the year you graduated high school? Neither do I. Well, I remember them if I hear them or see their names, but off the top of my head, I can only name a handful. That's why it's so cool that the iTunes Store has *Billboard* magazine's Hot 100 charts dating back to 1946, so all you have to do is find the one for the year you graduated from school, and 100 songs that sound really bad today will be listed (hey, don't laugh, when I graduated, the No. 1 song was "Shadow Dancing" by Andy Gibb). You can view *Billboard's* Hot 100 charts (and buy the songs listed on them) by starting at the iTunes Store homepage and clicking on the Browse button at the bottom-right of the iTunes window. In the Genre section, click on Charts; in the Chart section, click on *Billboard* Hot 100; and then in the Year section, click on the year you graduated. (I'm not telling you what year I graduated, but it could've been 1991. Hey, it could've been—if I had been a really, really, really bad student.) *Warning:* When you click on your year, you'll see a list of songs that will immediately elicit a verbal: "Oh, no way that song was No. 1."

Quickly Finding All of an Artist's Songs

If you see an artist you'd like to see more of (let's say you're searching for songs, and you happen to see a Willie Nelson song in the results—hey, Willie rocks), just click on the little gray circle with an arrow inside it right after the artist's name. Clicking on this takes you directly to a page where you'll find all of the artist's songs available in the iTunes Store. Some artists even have a "feature page" that will appear when you click on the little arrow; then you not only get the big fancy photo of the artist(s), but if you look around on this page you're also likely to find a Biography link, and sometimes a link to the artist's website or iTunes exclusives. Click on the Biography link and get some background info on the artist. Hey, it saves you a trip to the artist's website. Try this once, and you'll use it again and again.

---

iTip: iTunes in Other Countries

Want to take a peek at what the iTunes Store for Germany is like? Easy enough—just start at the iTunes Store homepage, and at the center of the main window, right near the bottom, click on the Choose Country pop-up menu, and a list will appear representing each of the iTunes Stores in the world. To see what another country's store is like (and see their top songs), just choose that country from the pop-up menu.

Emailing Your Uncovered Treasures

If you've just uncovered the coolest song in the iTunes Store, you can send a friend directly to that song. Just open your email program (while you still have the iTunes Store visible), and click-and-drag the song's album cover (or the song title, either will work) over into your opened email message. The song's iTunes Store URL will be pasted into your email, just like a regular Web link. All your friend has to do is click on that link, and she'll be taken right there. This is a great feature to use when your girlfriend/boyfriend breaks up with you. You can send her links to a bunch of "broken-hearted" breakup songs, like "Here Without You" by 3 Doors Down or "What Happened To Us?" by Hoobastank or the most obvious "The Breakup Song" by Greg Kihn—but I'm not sure that song will have the desired effect (the song name is good, but the message is weak if you're trying to get some broken-hearted sympathy).

---

iTip: iTunes Store Alerts

Once you've bought a bunch of classic songs from your favorite artists, wouldn't it be cool to know when they've introduced a new song? Don't worry—the iTunes Store tracks all this for you, and if you click on the My Alerts link (in the Quick Links section at the top of homepage's third column), it shows all the new songs released by artists you've already downloaded. In fact, while you're there, you can sign up to have the iTunes Store send you an email notification as soon as a new song from one of "your artists" is released.

Finding Out If You Already Have This Song

Okay, you're checking out some music on the iTunes Store and you come across a song you really like (let's say it's "Love Train" by Wolfmother), and you say to yourself, "Ya know, I really like that song. I wonder—do I already have it?" Well, wonder no more, because here's a very slick and very fast way to find out—hold the Option key (PC: Ctrl key) and click on the little gray arrow to the right of the artist's name in the iTunes Store. This jumps you out of the iTunes Store and directly to a list of the Wolfmother songs in *your* Music Library, so you can see if you've got it. Seriously, how cool is that— it leaves the iTunes Store and shows you which Wolfmother songs you've already got in *your* Music Library. I just think that's so cool (try it once and you'll see what I mean).

---

iTip: Completing an Album

If you've got a song or two from a particular album, you can have the iTunes Store "finish off" that album for you, by automatically finding the missing songs you need to complete the album, compiling them, and letting you buy and download them all at once. Just click on the Complete My Album link (under Quick Links, at the top of the third column on the homepage), and it shows all the albums that are eligible to be completed, which songs are required to complete them, and how much that would cost. Pretty handy, eh?

Buying Protected Songs

Most of the songs available in the iTunes Store are protected using digital rights management (called DRM for short), which is a limited form of digital copy protection, and by limited I mean it lets you make copies to your iPod and up to five other "authorized" machines (machines you authorize), but that's about it. This DRM is embedded into the songs, and it basically stops people from sharing these songs with their friends, or posting them for free download online, and by having it in place, it makes sure the artists get royalties from songs bought from the iTunes Store. The fact that Apple did this (include DRM in the songs it sells from the iTunes Store) is why so many record labels make their music available on iTunes, and that's part of the reason why the iTunes Store is far and away the most successful online music store in the world. So, by default, when you buy a song in the regular iTunes Store, you know it's protected with DRM. Just so ya know.

---

iTip: Artist Alert in the iTunes Store

If you like a particular artist, you can be emailed when he or she adds a new song (or album) to the iTunes Store. This feature is called Artist Alert, and to sign up for it, just do a search for your favorite artist, click on any album art to launch that album's page, and then on the right of the page, click on Alert Me. It's as easy as that.

Buying Unprotected Songs

Although since its beginning, all songs in the iTunes Store have been DRM-protected, in early 2007, Apple broke the mold by introducing unprotected music downloads with no restrictions on how you use the songs for your personal use (or which MP3 player you can play them on). These unrestricted songs are in a separate area called iTunes Plus, and you're getting the highest quality audio ever offered by Apple. To find them, click on the iTunes Plus link in the Quick Links section at the top of the right column on the iTunes Store homepage. *Note:* Not every song is available as an iTunes Plus unrestricted song, as only certain record companies agreed to offer their music without DRM, but the selection is growing and I imagine more and more record companies will start making their music available this way.

---

iTip: Upgrading Your Songs

When you click on the iTunes Plus link, iTunes will search through your current music collection, find which songs you already own that are also available as iTunes Plus, and it offers you the opportunity to upgrade those DRM versions to unrestricted songs (for 30¢ each). It tells you exactly how many songs qualify, and how much the total conversion will cost (in my collection, it found 16 songs, which it told me would cost only $4.20 to convert all 16). Music videos are also available for upgrade for 60¢ each.

Seeing the Big Cover!

If you buy songs from the iTunes Store, there's a little bonus: not only does it download the album art (so you can see it in the left-hand corner of the iTunes interface when you click the Show Artwork button—it's the fourth button from the left), but if you click directly on the album art, a separate floating window will appear with a huge version of the cover. Well, technically you could get either a huge or a medium version, depending on how long it's been since you downloaded the song from the iTunes Store, because the super-huge, almost-full-screen covers are a newer feature. Either way, it's fairly cool to see the covers at a much larger size.

---

iTip: Adding More Album Art

You can actually have more than one album cover per song (meaning there's an import cover, or an extended mix cover, or single cover, etc.). Just drag the cover you want from your Web browser (that means you found the album cover on the band's website) and drop it right over the cover that's there now. You'll notice little arrows will appear above your album art, so you can cycle over to see the different covers.

Why You Need to Back Up Your Purchased Songs

In the back of your mind you're probably thinking, "Hey, if my hard drive ever totally dies, I'm covered, because Apple keeps a history of all my iTunes purchases, and if that mega-crash day ever comes, I'll just drop Apple an email and they'll let me download all the purchased songs again, right?" Nope. If your hard drive dies, all of your purchased songs go right to the grave with it. Apple will *not* let you download them again without paying for them. That's why it's SO important to back up your purchased music. To do this, first click on Purchased in the Source list (on the left side of the iTunes window) to select it. Then click on the Burn Disc button in the bottom right-hand corner of the iTunes window. Insert a blank disc (when iTunes tells you to), then start-a-burnin'. Keep poppin' in new discs until all those songs are backed up to CD. Now, will Apple ever change its mind about this, since serious hard disk crashes are nearly an inevitability? Probably one day, but it hasn't happened yet, and until it does, you're not "covered." If you don't back up, one day you're almost certain to lose your entire iTunes Store investment. So…back it up now (step away from the book and start backing up).

A Source for Musical Inspiration

If you can't think of any songs to buy and you need a little inspiration, go to the iTunes Store homepage, and on the left side of the main window, click on Music, then scroll down and click on Celebrity Playlists. Apple has asked a number of celebrities to create and publish their own playlists, and often their suggestions for songs are very good. You can sort the listing by date added (to get the most recent celebrity playlists) or alphabetically by name using the pop-up menu in the top-right corner of the iTunes Store window. Once you find a musician or celebrity that interests you, just click on that person's photo to see his picks and, most importantly, a note on why he picked 'em. Best of all, because his picks are sold in the iTunes Store, you can hear a 30-second preview of each suggestion. This may sound a little corny, but if you give it a try, I think you'll be quite surprised at some of the cool music your favorite celebrities and bands are listening to.

---

iTip: Make Your Own iMix

Since Apple introduced iMix (which basically makes you the celebrity), you can publish your own playlists on the iTunes Store and share them with the world (so other people can buy your favorite songs). To create and publish your own iMix, just put together a playlist of your favorite songs within iTunes, then go under the File menu and choose Create an iMix. iTunes will connect to the iTunes Store and your iMix will be live. To see other people's iMixes (and rate them), go to the iTunes Store homepage, click on Music, and on the Music page, click on iMix on the left side of the window.

Setting Your Video Screen Size

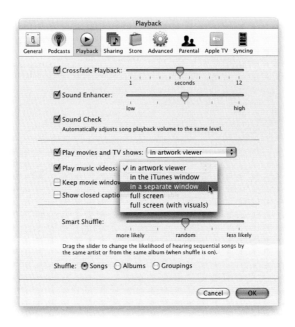

As I'm sure you know, the iTunes Store offers music videos, TV shows, movies, and movie trailers, but what you might not realize is that you have some control over how large these videos will appear onscreen within iTunes (in other words, it doesn't just have to appear in the tiny Artwork viewer). To choose how you want your video served up, just go to the iTunes Preferences (under the iTunes menu on a Mac; under the Edit menu on a Windows PC), and click on the Playback icon. Near the middle of the Playback preferences, you'll find a pop-up menu that lets you choose your preferred playback size for movies and TV shows, and a separate preference setting for the size music videos will be displayed. You can choose to play videos in the main iTunes window, in a separate window (which basically shows the video in a floating, resizable QuickTime player window), or in full-screen mode (with or without visuals), which can be a bit dicey depending on the quality of the video you're watching and the size of your screen. Just choose your desired playback size from the pop-up menus (shown above) and click OK.

Keeping Naughty Videos from the Kids

Okay, so you bought your 12-year-old son an iPod for Christmas, and you gave him an iTunes gift certificate so he could buy some music and videos from the iTunes Store. Here's the thing—there's nothing to stop him from downloading explicit audio and video podcasts, music with lyrics so nasty they'd make Snoop Dogg blush, and even R-rated movies. So, what's to keep your child from getting his hands on all this naughty stuff? You are. Well, you using the parental controls built into iTunes, which are designed to let you decide to keep naughty stuff out of your kid's iPod. You do this in the iTunes Preferences (press Command-, [comma] on the Mac, or Ctrl-, on the PC to bring up the Preferences dialog) by clicking on the Parental icon at the top-right side of the dialog to bring up the parental controls (shown above). Here you can choose to restrict entire sources of content (like podcasts, radio, etc.), or to restrict music downloads in the iTunes Store based on the Explicit rating tagged to adult content, or to restrict TV shows and movies based on their ratings. Once you make your choices (this is important), click on the Lock icon (as shown) to lock and password protect these changes, or your 12-year-old will quickly disable those restrictions (never underestimate a 12-year-old boy on a computer). Now click OK, and you gain some modicum of peace of mind.

Controlling Your Spending

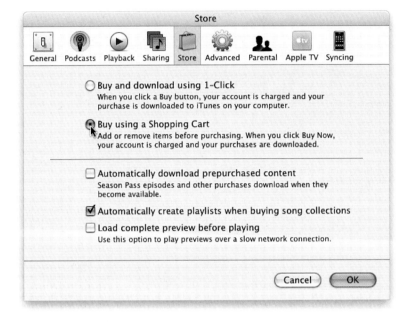

With songs being only 99¢, they just seem so cheap that it's easy to buy songs—until the Visa bill comes and you're shocked at how many 99¢ charges there are. Rather than just blindly buying songs one at a time, turn on the iTunes Store's Shopping Cart feature. Go to the iTunes Preferences (under the iTunes menu on the Mac; under the Edit menu on a Windows PC). Just click on the Store icon at the top of the dialog, and then choose Buy Using a Shopping Cart. This changes the Buy Song button to Add Song. Now when you click the Add Song button, songs will wind up listed on your Shopping Cart page at checkout time. None of these songs is downloaded or charged to your account until you actually press the Buy Now button at the bottom of your Shopping Cart page. To go back to your freewheeling, spend-like-a-drunken-sailor ways, return to the Store Preferences and check Buy and Download Using 1-Click.

Keeping an Eye on Your Spending

Although Apple knows exactly how much money you've been spending recently at the iTunes Store, you might want to know yourself (so you can prepare items that will need to be pawned). To find out how much you've spent, just click on the Account button (the one that shows your email address) in the upper right-hand corner of the iTunes Store. (If you're not already logged in, it'll ask you for your username and password.) On your Account Information page, you'll find a button called Purchase History. Click it and get ready to freak out as all the purchases, and their costs, are listed one after another. When you've wiped away your tears, press the Done button, because "you're done."

---

iTip: Log Out If You Leave

If you're using the iTunes Store at work and you duck out for lunch, someone else might want to duck into your office, buy a few songs on your dime, download them to his iPod, and then head back to his cubicle before you return. You won't know what happened until your Visa bill arrives. So, when you know you're stepping away for a few minutes, click on the Account button (the one that shows your email address) at the top right of the iTunes Store window and choose Sign Out from the dialog that appears. That way, no one can come in and abuse your account while you're out. When you come back, just log back in and continue downloading more songs on company time.

Setting Up an iTunes Allowance

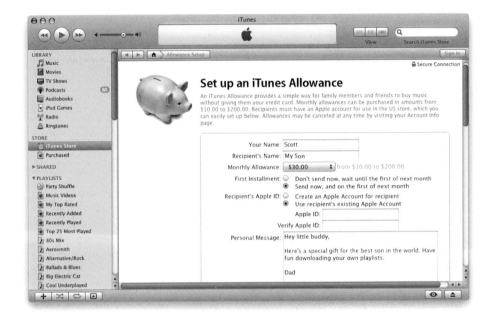

Want a high-tech way to spoil your kids? How about giving them an iTunes Store download allowance? It's scarily convenient, because once you choose how much they get each month, it's all automated from there: The iTunes Store credits their account each month and charges your credit card—it's downright eerie. Now, although I'm poking some fun at it here, when you think about it, this is much safer than giving them your (or their own) credit card, because *you* determine exactly how much they can spend. Here's how to set your kids up: From the iTunes Store homepage, in the list of Quick Links on the right side, click on Buy iTunes Gifts. On this page, click on the Set Up Allowance Now link. This brings up the Allowance setup page, where you can give your child an allowance of up to $200 a month. (By the way, if you choose $200, your next call should be to a therapist.) Once you've entered your information, click Continue. When your child signs into his account, Apple will deliver the "good news." How personal and folksy.

---

iTip: iTunes Store Gift Certificates

Another of my favorite iTunes Store features is the ability to email or mail a friend a gift certificate for the Store. Just go to the iTunes Store, sign in, and click on Buy iTunes Gifts. If you're redeeming one, click on the Redeem link instead, and the iTunes Store will give you credits in the amount of the gift certificate. Your running balance will appear in the upper right-hand corner of the iTunes Store window. By the way, you can buy certificates in person at the Apple Store in the mall, too.

Stop Unauthorized People from Buying Music

Most songs you download from the iTunes Store can be copied to just five computers (thanks to a built-in digital rights protection scheme called "Fair Play"), so theoretically, you could buy a song on your desktop machine, then authorize your laptop as your second machine, and then authorize your computer at work as your third, and you'd still have two computers left to authorize (plus you can copy songs to as many of your iPods as you'd like—fair enough). You can also buy more songs from these five machines and charge them to your account. But that also means if you sell your computer or give it to someone else (maybe someone else within your company will wind up using your old machine), you definitely want to "deauthorize" it, or they may be able to buy songs too—and charge them to you. To deauthorize your computer, go under the Store menu in iTunes and choose Deauthorize Computer. When the dialog appears, click OK and the computer you're currently using will be deactivated. *Note:* Just erasing and reformatting a hard drive will not deauthorize a computer—you have to deauthorize it manually, as shown here.

Sharing iTunes Store Music

If you're on a network (at work, at home, at school, etc.), you can share your playlists with other people on the network. That's right; they can play your songs in your playlists from right within their copy of iTunes. The only downside is that they won't get to hear songs you bought from the iTunes Store—when those purchased songs appear in a playlist, iTunes skips over them automatically (to, once again, protect the copyrights of the music you bought). If you want someone on your network to be able to hear your iTunes Store music, you'll have to "authorize" his computer. Just go to his computer, log in with your iTunes Store username (email address) and password, then go under the Advanced menu and choose Authorize Computer. (*Note:* This computer becomes one of the five that you're allowed to authorize under your iTunes Store account.)

---

iTip: Gift a Song

If you run across a song you really, really like, you can actually buy the song, and send it to a friend as a gift. (Your friend will be emailed a link where she can download your thoughtful gift.) Here's how to send a song, or an entire album (or a music video), to a friend as a gift: Go to the iTunes Store and find the artist's page for the album that includes the song you want. Then, near the top, click the Gift This Music link. This takes you to a page where you can choose individual songs from that artist—just click the Gift Song button beside the song you want to send, then follow the step-by-step instructions for sending it to your friend. See, you do care, don't you?

Speeding Up Sharing and Previews

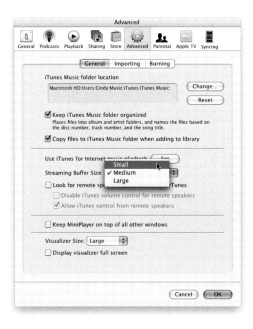

If you're on a local network, chances are you've got a direct and pretty speedy connection to that network. If that's the case, you can speed things up even more by tweaking an iTunes preference that will accelerate the loading of both the iTunes Store previews, and of shared playlists across your network. What you're doing is just shrinking the iTunes Streaming Buffer Size, meaning it buffers a smaller amount of info before it begins playing, so you see previews faster and hear shared songs faster. If that all sounds confusing, it should. So, does it really matter what kind of magic goes into making iTunes run faster? No? Then great, do this: Go to iTunes Preferences (found under the iTunes menu on a Mac; the Edit menu on a Windows PC), then click on the Advanced icon and choose General. From the pop-up menu for Streaming Buffer Size, choose Small, and now things will move faster. See, that was fairly painless, eh, Bunky?

Got a Slow Connection? Get Better Previews

If you have a slow-speed (dial-up) connection to the Internet, you're probably suffering a frustrating version of one of the coolest iTunes Store features—the ability to hear a 30-second preview of any song. The problem is that these previews stream, and because of the slow speed of your dial-up connection, those audio streams often skip, are choppy, and sometimes are out-and-out painful to listen to. But it doesn't have to be that way. Just buy a high-speed connection! (Kidding.) Actually, there's something you can do—stop the streaming. That's right, there's a preference that stops the streaming audio and instead loads the entire music preview before it plays. That way, there's no chopping, no skipping—just clean, pure previews, baby! Here's how to turn it on: Go to the iTunes Preferences (on a Mac, it's under the iTunes menu; on a Windows PC, it's under the Edit menu) and when the dialog appears, click on the Store icon. Then turn on the checkbox labeled Load Complete Preview Before Playing. That's it—it'll take a little extra time while the preview is downloading, but once it does, it'll sound perfect. *Note:* Turn on this option only if you're using a telephone line dial-up connection. If you have a cable modem, T1, or DSL connection, you should leave this turned off.

Moving Your Music to Another Computer

The iPod "Scott Kelby's iPod" is synced with another iTunes library. An iPod can be synced with only one iTunes library at a time. What would you like to do?

"Erase and Sync" replaces the contents of this iPod with the contents of this iTunes library.

"Transfer Purchases" copies iTunes Store purchases this computer is authorized to play from this iPod to this iTunes library.

☐ Do not ask me again

(Cancel)   (**Transfer Purchases**) (Erase and Sync)

If you want to transfer music or videos that you've purchased in the iTunes Store to another computer, the fastest and easiest way is to move them using your iPod. Here's how it's done: Apple allows you to authorize up to five computers to play your purchased video and music contents from the iTunes Store. To move this purchased music from one authorized computer to another, you use your iPod (by the way, it just moves your music and videos purchased from the iTunes Store, not any music you imported from CDs or any other way). Once your purchased music (and videos) has been downloaded onto your iPod, just plug your iPod into another one of your authorized computers and a dialog will appear asking you if you want to transfer your purchased videos and music to this other authorized computer. If for some reason that dialog doesn't appear, just go under the File menu, choose Transfer Purchases from iPod, and it does the rest. By the way, if you're not sure how to authorize a computer to play your purchased music and videos, read the tip below.

---

iTip: Automatic Authorizing

Authorizing is an automatic thing: if you plug in your iPod to another one of your computers (like a laptop for instance), a dialog appears letting you know that this isn't an authorized computer, but as long as you haven't used up your five-computer limit, it will allow you to authorize that computer right there on the spot. Feel the power!

Allowing Multiple Simultaneous Downloads

When you buy songs or videos from the iTunes Store, they download in the order you purchased them. However, if you're on a serious buying spree, there's an option you'll want to know about that lets you download multiple purchases simultaneously, instead of one-by-one in order. To get to this option, you have to be downloading a song, because the checkbox that turns this option on is actually found in the downloading window itself. Once a song is downloading, click on Downloads under Stores in the far-left side of the iTunes window, and you'll see this option near the bottom of that window.

Do Your iTunes Store Downloading Later

iTunes lets you manage your downloads, so if you're downloading a bunch of songs (maybe a whole album) or a movie, you can pause your download and start again later, when it's more convenient. This is incredibly helpful if you started downloading something, and then you have to leave before the downloading is done. No sweat—you can just pick up later, right where you left off. This download manager only appears when you're downloading music, videos, or games from the iTunes Store so you won't see it in your Source list until you're actually downloading. When you are downloading from the Store, the Downloads link will appear in your Store section directly below Purchased. Click on it, and it displays a list of the items you're currently downloading. It can download up to three simultaneous items, but if you've got more than that lined up to download, you can drag the queued-up downloads into the order you want them downloaded (so that way, if you can't wait to download Fergie's new song, you can move it up higher in the queue). If you want to pause a download in progress, just click the little Pause button that appears to the right of the status bar. To resume that download, click the circular button that now appears in its place. To pause all your downloads, click the Pause All button in the bottom-right corner of the main window. To resume all your downloads at once, click the Resume All button. Once all your music (and/or videos) are downloaded, this Downloads link will disappear.

iTunes Will Grab That Album Art for You

When you buy a song from the iTunes Store, it comes with album art automatically, but if you didn't get a song there (let's say you imported songs from an audio CD), and you wanted the accompanying album art, you used to have to go searching around the Web to hopefully find the cover art, and then manually drag it into iTunes. It was kind of a pain. Of course today, we laugh at how they used to get album art "in the old days," because in most cases iTunes will automatically go online, find the album art, and load it right in there for us. So, unless iTunes simply can't find the art, you're set. However, every once in a while—it happens. Maybe you didn't enter the proper song name, or you misspelled a song title, or you just like music so obscure that even iTunes, with the iTunes Store's vast database of album art, doesn't recognize your musical brilliance (see how I threw you a bone there?), then you'll have to do it "the old fashioned way" which is detailed earlier in this chapter.

---

iTip: Getting CD Artwork

If you import some songs from a CD, and iTunes doesn't grab the cover art for you, just go under the Advanced menu and choose Get Album Artwork, and it'll take it there from.

Creating a Wish List in iTunes

If you've found some music, TV shows, or movies you'd like to buy, but you're a little strapped for cash right now, you can create an iTunes Store wish list. Theoretically, this is stuff you want to buy one day, but ideally you'd have a friend or relative buy it for you, right? (You moocher.) Here's how to set up yours: Just create a new playlist (click on the Create a Playlist button in the bottom-left corner of iTunes), and when your new playlist appears in the Source list, name it "Wish List." Then, when you're browsing in the iTunes Store and you run across a song, TV show, or movie you'd like to add to your wish list, just click-and-drag that item into your Wish List playlist. This brings the direct link (including the 30-second preview) from the iTunes Store into your wish list. That makes it easy when you finally do decide to pony up the money for one of those items. However, buying a song doesn't remove it from your wish list—you have to manually go and delete it (and remember, that doesn't remove it from your main Library, just from that playlist). (*Note:* You can only drag items to a playlist from an iTunes Store individual preview list. If you want to add an entire album of music, a movie, or TV show season, you'll need to create a Wish List folder on your Desktop. Then you can drag the album art, or movie or TV show poster, to this folder.)

Chapter Eleven

Imaginary Player
Playlists and Smart Playlists

Hey, it's not easy finding a song with the word "playlist" in it. Or a movie. Or a TV show. So, after doing some searching, I got as close as I was going to get with the song "Imaginary Player" by Jay-Z. Now, in the iTunes Store, there are two different versions of this song—one with the Explicit lyrics warning and one with the Clean label. Normally, I just go with the Clean version, because I'm a wholesome, family man myself. (However, one time I actually got "burned" when downloading the Clean version of a song. It was the song "1985" by Bowling for Soup. My wife heard the song on Radio Disney, told me about it, and when I found it on the iTunes Store, it had both Explicit and Clean versions, so of course I downloaded the Clean version for my son's playlist on my iPod. However, Apple's definition of Clean is obviously different than Radio Disney's. For example, on the Radio Disney version of the song, the second verse goes: "She was gonna be an actress. She was gonna be a star. She was gonna shake it, on the hood of Whitesnake's car." The "shake it" part's a little suggestive, but it's certainly not explicit. However, in the Clean version I downloaded, instead it says: "She was gonna shake her ass, on the hood of Whitesnake's car." Unsuspecting, I played it in front of my son, only once mind you, but of course he's memorized that line verbatim. Kids!) Anyway, this chapter isn't about the explicit version of either Jay-Z's or Bowling for Soup's song, but if it were, I'd probably sell a lot more books.

Creating Your Own Playlists

Playlists are like your own custom collections of songs (like you might have a playlist of mellow music, or driving music, or big-hair bands of the '80s, etc.). Creating playlists takes just two steps. The first is to click the Create a Playlist button at the bottom left-hand corner of the iTunes window. Your new playlist will appear in the Source list along the left side of the iTunes window, and the name field for your playlist will already be highlighted so you can name it. Type in a name and press Return (PC: Enter) to lock it in. Now, in the Source list, click on Music under Library so you can see all your songs in the iTunes window, then simply drag-and-drop songs from your Music Library onto your new playlist's icon. To see the songs in your playlist (or to play your playlist), just click on the playlist in the Source list.

Removing Songs from a Playlist

If a playlist includes a song that just plain shouldn't be there (for example, if "Silent Morning" by Noel winds up on your 80s Rock Mix playlist), you can remove it fast by clicking on it and pressing the Delete (PC: Backspace) key on your keyboard. Now, what if a song like "Between You and Me'" or "Party Your Body" somehow wound up on that playlist as well? You can remove multiple bad songs by Command-clicking (PC: Ctrl-clicking) on them and then pressing Delete (or you can Control-click [PC: Right-click] on any of those selected songs and choose Delete from the contextual menu that appears), instantly wiping their innate lameness from your playlist. (*Note:* This won't remove the songs from your iTunes Music Library; it will only remove them from the playlist.)

---

iTip: Temporarily Skipping Songs

If you've got a song in one of your playlists that you don't want to delete, but you don't want to hear it right now, you can just temporarily skip over it by turning off the checkbox that appears directly before the song's name (only checked songs will be played when playing a playlist). If you later decide you want to hear that song in the playlist, just turn on the checkbox beside it.

Removing an Entire Playlist

If you've created a playlist, and you just don't want it anymore (let's say you created a Christmas playlist and now it's February), just Control-click (PC: Right-click) on the playlist in the Source list on the left-hand side of the iTunes window and choose Delete from the contextual menu. That's it—it's gone. Or even better: just click on the playlist to select it in the Source list and press the Delete (PC: Backspace) key. *Note:* Only the playlist is gone—it doesn't remove the songs from your main iTunes Music Library.

Another Way to Create Playlists

Throughout this book, when we talk about creating a regular playlist, we generally talk about dragging-and-dropping songs from your Music Library into your playlist, but there's another quick way to create a custom playlist. Just Command-click (PC: Ctrl-click) on all the songs in your Music Library that you want in your playlist, and then go under the File menu and choose New Playlist from Selection (or press Command-Shift-N [PC: Ctrl-Shift-N]). All the selected songs will be gathered into a new playlist, and it will appear in the Source list with its name field already highlighted, so all you have to do is type in your new playlist's name and press Return (PC: Enter).

---

iTip: Opening in a Separate Window

When you click on a playlist, that playlist appears in the main iTunes window, replacing whatever was visible before (like perhaps your Music Library). However, if you'd like a playlist to open in its own separate floating window (leaving your original window still open and untouched), instead of clicking on your playlist, just double-click on its icon or to the right of its name in the Source list.

Making a List of Your Playlists

If you'd like a printed list of one (or more) of your playlists and their contents (hey, don't laugh—this is handy if your hard drive has a major crash and you haven't backed up in a while…or ever), iTunes can make one for you. First, in the Source list on the left side of the iTunes window, Control-click (PC: Right-click) on the playlist that you want to print and from the pop-up menu that appears, choose Export Song List. A Save dialog will appear, so choose where you want to save the file on your hard disk, then click Save. iTunes exports your playlist as a tab-delimited text file, which you can open with a spreadsheet or database program like Microsoft Excel, FileMaker Pro, etc., and then print out the file.

Combining Two Playlists into One

If you realize that you have two similar playlists (like one called Big Hair Bands and one called 80s Rock Mix), you can combine them into one playlist (which you could name 80s Hair Bands) by simply clicking-and-dragging one playlist onto another playlist, right within the Source list. Now, it's important to note that dragging the Big Hair Bands playlist into the 80s Rock Mix playlist creates a combined playlist (copying one playlist into another, which by the way will cause any duplicate songs that were in both lists to appear twice, so you may want to delete the duplicates). Luckily, iTunes doesn't erase the Big Hair Bands playlist. It's still there—with all its Bon Jovi rockness.

Finding the Length of Your Playlist

Want to know how long (in days, hours, minutes, etc.) one of your playlists is (or for that matter, how long it would take to play your entire Music Library)? Click on any playlist (or your Music Library), and then look at the bottom center of your iTunes window. You'll see how many songs are in your selected playlist, and how long it would take you to play them all. If you actually click on the time, you can toggle between a generic hour timeframe or see it spelled out for you in hours, minutes, and seconds.

---

iTip: Estimate Size Before Burning

Be sure to make note of the playlist's total size. This really comes in handy when burning playlists to CDs, because this little nugget of info will save you a ton of frustration by allowing you to estimate the total size of your files before you even begin the burning process. (Note: Keep in mind that the total size listed is for your compressed files, not the uncompressed AIF files that'll automatically be burned onto the audio CD; hence the word estimate.*)*

Putting Your Songs in Your Order

There are a number of different ways to have iTunes automatically sort the songs in one of your playlists (e.g., alphabetically by Name or Artist, by Genre, Rating, etc.), but what if you want to arrange the songs manually so they're in *your* order? You can do this by simply dragging the songs into the order you want, but this "drag-and-drop" arranging can only be done within playlists, not in your main Music Library. Also, to sort the songs manually like this, you have to click in the very first column header from the left to make it the active column (it's called the Track Number column, but its name doesn't appear); otherwise, if one of the other columns (like Artist) is highlighted, the songs will already be auto-sorted by artist, right? Right! So click in the far-left column, and then you can begin sorting. Oh yeah, one last thing—if you have the Shuffle option turned on (the second button from the left at the bottom-left corner of the iTunes window), it won't let you manually sort. So if you're in a playlist, and you've got the first column highlighted, and you still can't sort, it's probably because Shuffle is turned on. Turn it off by clicking on the Shuffle button, and you're in business.

Rearranging Your Column Order

If you're not happy with the default order of the columns (for example, if you'd prefer that the Artist column was the third column, right after the Name column), you can make it happen. Just click-and-hold the Artist column's header and drag it to the left, until it appears right after the Name column (you'll see a "ghost" image of your column as you move it, so it's pretty simple to move it where you want it). Now that you know how it's done, you can arrange the columns in any order you want (except for the Track Number and Name columns—those are stuck there permanently, but besides those two, you can arrange your columns any way you want).

Changing the Sort Name

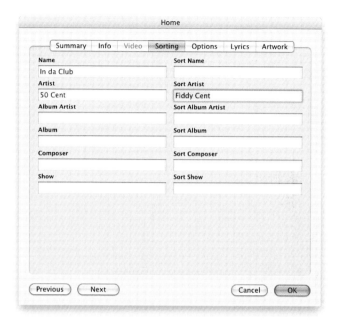

If you don't like the way iTunes sorts your songs, you can give them a hidden custom name or artist name, just for sorting purposes (the name will appear the same to you, but it will now be sorted the way you want). For example, if you sort your playlists by Artist, and you have a song by 50 Cent (It's "In da Club," isn't it? I knew it!), it will wind up at the bottom of your list. This is a problem if you go looking for it under "F" for "Fiddy Cent" (at least that's where I'd look). So, to create a hidden sorting name, you click on the file and press Command-I (PC: Ctrl-I), and when the Info window appears, click on the Sorting tab. It's split into two sides: the left side is what you see in iTunes (the real artist, real name, etc.) and the right side is what iTunes will actually use when sorting. So, in the right side Artist field, you'd type in "Fiddy Cent" and click OK. Now 50 Cent will appear sorted under "F." Pretty slick little feature, eh?

Rating Your Songs (and Why You Should)

Even though you probably like all the songs you've imported into iTunes (or you wouldn't have imported them, right?), there are some songs in your Music Library that you like better than others. In fact, there are probably some of your all-time favorites, some you like pretty well, and some you just like okay. Well, you can—and should—give each song a rating (using a one- to five-star rating system). One reason to rate songs is that once you've given songs a high rating (four to five stars), iTunes automatically adds your top-rated songs into a default Smart Playlist named My Top Rated (depending on your version of iTunes). So anytime you want to hear just your favorite songs, there's already a playlist (that updates live) ready for you. Plus, you can sort your songs using the Rating column (by just clicking on it), and you can create your own custom Smart Playlists based on your ratings (see next page). To rate a song, just click directly on the song, then click in the left-hand side of the Rating column (found in the main iTunes window) and drag to the right. As you drag, stars will highlight, so click until you see the first star and drag to the right until the fifth star is "lit." To "unlight" a star, drag back to the left. You can also rate by Control-clicking (PC: Right-clicking) on a song, and then choosing your rating from the contextual menu. *Note:* If you're on a Mac, you can even rate the song that's playing from the Mac's Dock by clicking-and-holding on the iTunes Dock icon and choosing your rating from there; on a Windows PC, Right-click the iTunes icon in the Navigation Area on the Taskbar and choose Rating.

Putting Your Ratings to Work

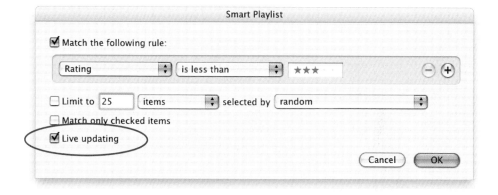

Now that you've rated your songs, here's how to create a Smart Playlist using those ratings: Since iTunes automatically creates a Smart Playlist of your top-rated songs, why not
create a playlist of your 25 lowest-rated songs (just for the sheer variety of it)? To do that,
choose New Smart Playlist from the iTunes File menu, and in the dialog that appears, from
the first pop-up menu choose Rating; from the second menu choose Is Less Than; and
click in the third field to choose three stars, then click OK. That's it—you have a new Smart
Playlist of nothing but your lowest-rated songs. Oh, ensure the Live Updating checkbox is
turned on (it should be on by default), and as you rate new songs with a one- or two-star
rating, they'll be added to this Smart Playlist automatically.

---

iTip: Smart Playlist Updating

*Since iTunes tracks so much information about your songs and about your song–playing
habits (it knows which songs you've played the most, the rankings of those songs, etc.),
iTunes can make Smart Playlists based on these stats or based on your own personal preferences. What's cool is that Smart Playlists feature live updating, so if you make a change
(like playing a song, changing the rating of a song, or playing a song a bunch), these Smart
Playlists update automatically. But the real power comes when you create your own Smart
Playlists, which also can update automatically if you'd like. Once you make your own—even
once—the power of Smart Playlists will become clear, my young apprentice.*

Using Genres to Create a Smart Playlist

Once you've assigned custom genres to your iTunes songs, you can make some wicked Smart Playlists. For example, I wanted to create a "car mix" that would be the equivalent of a radio station that played nothing but my songs, in random order, with no commercials. But I didn't want it to include my son's songs (I let him have a playlist on my iPod), or any Christmas songs, or any songs I use in video editing, or...well, you get the idea. So I made a Smart Playlist by holding the Option key (PC: Alt key), then clicking on the Create a Playlist button in the bottom left-hand corner of the iTunes window. This brings up the Smart Playlist dialog. At the top, under Match the Following Rule, I chose Genre from the first pop-up menu. From the second menu, I chose Is Not, then in the text field I entered the genre I didn't want ("Christmas Songs"). I then clicked on the + (plus sign) button to the right of the field to add another rule. I chose the same pop-up menus, and in the field I entered "My Son's Music." I did it again for "Video Background Music," "Conference Music," and "Radio Disney Music." Then I finally ensured Live Updating was turned on, and when I clicked OK, my "Car Mix" Smart Playlist was created, without any of the songs I didn't want. Now when I add a new song (that's labeled with any other genre than the ones I blocked), it's automatically added to my Car Mix Smart Playlist.

Create a Smart Playlist of Your Least-Played Songs

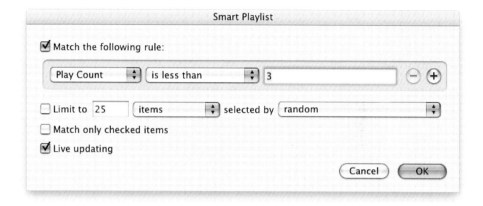

If you have thousands of songs on your iPod (or even hundreds for that matter), there are probably tunes on there that you haven't listened to much. Want a great idea for a Smart Playlist? Have iTunes create one made up of songs you haven't played recently (or at all). Start by holding the Option key (PC: Alt key) and clicking on the Create a Playlist button in the bottom-left corner of the iTunes window. When the Smart Playlist dialog appears, under Match the Following Rule, from the first pop-up menu choose Play Count. From the second menu, choose Is Less Than, and then in the blank field type "3" (or however many times you'd like, but keep it a low number). Make sure Live Updating is turned on, then click OK. A new Smart Playlist will be created of your least-played songs, and as you hear these songs more than three times (or however many times you specified), they'll automatically drop off the Smart Playlist thanks to the Live Updating option. You could also do a variation on this by choosing Last Played in the first field, choosing Is Before in the second field, then in the text field entering a date from a few months back. When you click OK, iTunes will create a Smart Playlist made up of songs you haven't heard in months.

A Smart Playlist for Short Trips

If you only live 10 minutes from your job (lucky you), you probably don't want to listen to one long song all the way to work, right? So why not create a Smart Playlist of just short songs? Here's how: Option-click (PC: Alt-click) on the Create a Playlist button to create a Smart Playlist. When the dialog appears, from the first pop-up menu choose Time; from the second pop-up menu choose Is Less Than; and in the text field enter "3:00." Now, when you play this Smart Playlist on your iPod on the way to work, you'll hear around three full songs, and you'll be at least one-third of the way through the fourth.

---

iTip: Songs You Heard a Week Ago

Want another Smart Playlist idea? How about this one—want to hear the same songs you heard exactly one week ago? Well, when you create your Smart Playlist, in the first pop-up menu, choose Last Played; in the second menu choose Is; and in the text field enter the date exactly one week ago today. A new Smart Playlist will be created with just the songs you heard exactly seven days ago. By the way, you might as well name this Smart Playlist "Déjà Vu." Hey, it's just an idea.

Get This Party Started with Party Shuffle

Another cool iTunes feature Apple added back in 2004 is the Party Shuffle. Rather than just choosing random songs (as the regular Shuffle command does), Party Shuffle is more likely to play songs that you've ranked highly or that you play often, so basically it plays more of your favorite songs than a standard random shuffle would. In fact, you can pretty much force Party Shuffle to favor your highly rated songs by clicking on Party Shuffle in the Source list on the left side of the iTunes window. When the Party Shuffle options appear at the bottom of the iTunes window, choose Play Higher Rated Songs More Often. But your "party control" doesn't end there. Other differences between Party Shuffle and a regular shuffle include: you can see what's already been played; you can see what's coming up next; and you have lots of control over it. You can choose to skip a song, delete it, move it higher in the playlist, etc., using the controls at the bottom of the iTunes window. So, Party Shuffle compiles the songs into a list, but as "party DJ," you really have the final say as to what gets played and when.

Party Shuffling from a Playlist

This is a great way to save time when you're making a Party Shuffle: base the new shuffle on a pre-existing playlist. For example, instead of the default of having Party Shuffle just pull random songs from your Music Library, have it pull from just a particular playlist. So let's say that you're having a theme party (like disco night); you can have Party Shuffle be the DJ by pulling random songs from your Disco playlist. Here's how it's done: When you click on Party Shuffle, the shuffled songs appear in the main window, but if you look at the bottom of the window (where the Party Shuffle controls now appear), you'll see a Source pop-up menu (which by default is set to Music). Choose the playlist you want to base your Party Shuffle on from this list, and you're set.

---

iTip: Rating an Album

Besides just rating individual songs, you can also assign ratings to albums by going under the View menu, choosing View Options, then turning on the checkbox for Album Rating, which adds a new Album Rating column to your iTunes window. If you use this column to rate an album, any songs you have that were on that album will now all share that same rating. If you rate your songs individually, it will automatically calculate an average rating based on the individual songs you did rate.

Making the Random Shuffle More Random

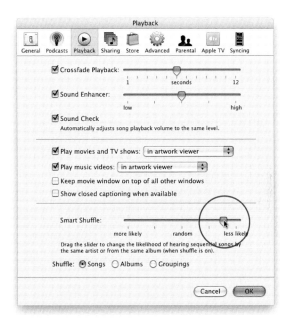

One of my friends once joked that Apple's Shuffle feature was the most predictable random device ever created. Sometimes he could even guess the next song while Shuffling (eerie, I know). Anyway, despite my friend's "next song" premonitions, apparently he wasn't the only one getting "messages from beyond," as the Shuffle feature does seem to have a preference for which artists it likes, and it does seem to play those artists more, even playing songs from the same artist back-to-back. Although technically that should be a rare occurrence, in reality it seems to happen more often than the odds would dictate if it were truly random. But we're not here to debate the randomness of the Shuffle feature; we're here to show you how to influence the randomness of the Shuffle. You do this in the iTunes Preferences by clicking on the Playback icon (up top) and then dragging the Smart Shuffle slider (shown above) either to the left, to increase your chance of hearing multiple songs in a row from the same artist, or to the right to reduce the chance (as I've done here).

Cutting Playlist Clutter with Playlist Folders

It's fairly easy to get sucked into "playlist mania" and before you know it you have 1,600 playlists—one for every mood, every occasion, every genre, every band, for every possible road trip, for…(well, you get the idea). You know you've got a problem when it takes you 11 minutes to scroll through your Source list. Anyway, if you need to bring some sanity to your playlist collection, in iTunes (version 5 and higher) you can add Playlist Folders in the Source list to organize all your playlists with a common theme in one place. For example, you could have a Folder named "Parties" and inside that you could store all the playlists you use at parties (your Rave mix, Burning Man mix, impromptu Vegas hotel room party mix, Diddy party mix, limo party mix, etc.). That way, they're all tucked away in just one folder. If you want to see them all individually again, just expand the folder (as shown above). To create a Playlist Folder, just go under the File menu and choose New Folder. The new folder will appear in the Source list, so you can easily drag-and-drop related playlists right into this folder.

---

iTip: Playing a Folder

Once you've put multiple playlists into one folder, you can then "play the folder" and it will just play the playlists in that folder. So, you could put all your rock playlists in one folder, and play them all at once by just choosing that folder. And in case you were wondering—yes, you can have subfolders (a folder within a folder).

Smart Playlist Idea for DJs

Let's say you're going to be the DJ at a party next week using your iPod. Obviously, you're going to need a lot of dance songs, but you're also going to need a playlist of slow songs. Using a Smart Playlist, you can gather all the slow songs you need pretty quickly. Just go through your Music Library and Command-click (PC: Ctrl-click) on every slow song you think you might want to use. Once you've gotten all the slow songs selected, press Command-I (PC: Ctrl-I) to bring up the Multiple Item Information dialog. In the Comments field, type in the words "Slow Songs" and click OK to add that comment to each selected song. Now, go under the File menu and choose New Smart Playlist. When the Smart Playlist dialog appears, from the first pop-up menu choose Comment; in the second menu choose Is; and in the text field enter "Slow Songs." Click OK and all the slow songs will be in their own playlist. Now do the same for all your dance songs—add the comment "Dance Songs" to each one, then make a Dance Songs Smart Playlist the same way.

Smart Playlist Idea: No Explicit Lyrics

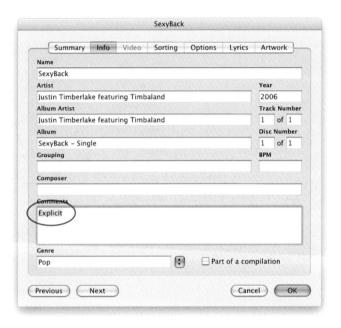

If you have a playlist that holds a lot of current music, you can almost bet that some songs are going to have explicit lyrics (Apple warns which iTunes Store songs have explicit lyrics by putting the word "Explicit" in red beside the song's name). For example, there are explicit lyrics on songs from recent albums by well-known artists like Korn, Motley Crue, Eminem, Nelly, and Justin Timberlake, and if some of these artists are your favorites, then it's likely you've downloaded some songs with explicit lyrics. Now, although you might enjoy these lyrics (sicko), you might not want these explicit songs blaring from your car stereo when your 7-year-old is in the backseat. The solution? A Smart Playlist of your favorite songs that automatically excludes any songs with explicit lyrics. The first step is "tagging" your songs with a keyword when you download them. When you download an explicit song, immediately click on the song, press Command-I (PC: Ctrl-I) and in the Get Info dialog, click on the Info tab. In the Comments field, type the word "Explicit," and then click OK. Now go under the File menu and choose New Smart Playlist. When the dialog appears, from the first pop-up menu choose Playlist; in the second menu choose Is; and in the third menu choose the playlist with all your favorite songs (including the ones with explicit lyrics). Then click the + (plus sign) button to add another line of criteria. In the first pop-up menu choose Comments; in the second menu choose Does Not Contain; and in the text field type "Explicit." Now click OK to create a new playlist with all your favorite songs, except the ones with explicit lyrics.

Smart Playlist Idea: Good '80s Songs Instantly

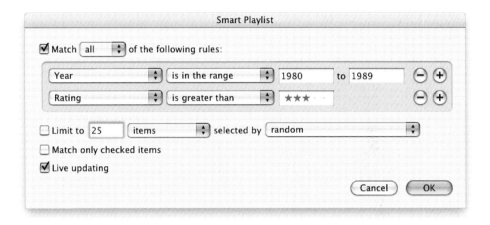

Okay, you want a list of nothing but your favorite songs from the 1980s. Here's what you do: Go under the File menu and choose New Smart Playlist. When the dialog appears, in the first pop-up menu choose Year; in the second pop-up menu choose Is in the Range; and in the two fields to the right enter "1980" and "1989." Then click the + (plus sign) button to add another line of criteria. From the first pop-up menu choose Rating; in the second pop-up menu choose Is Greater Than; in the star field choose three stars; and then click OK. Now you've got a playlist of just the songs in your iTunes Music Library published during the '80s, but since they have a four-star or higher rating, it's just your highest-rated (favorite) songs. Not bad, eh?

---

iTip: A Playlist of Your New Music

Want to hear a playlist of just your latest music? It's Smart Playlist time—go under the File menu and choose New Smart Playlist. When the dialog appears, from the first pop-up menu choose Date Added; from the second choose Is In The Last; in the text field enter "30"; choose Days in the fourth pop-up menu; and click OK. A new Smart Playlist will appear with only your new songs. If you want to tweak it even more (so this new list is made up of only your highest-rated new songs), click the + (plus sign) button to add another line of criteria, and then from the first pop-up menu choose Rating; in the second menu choose Is Greater Than; in the star field choose four stars; and then click OK.

Smart Playlist Idea: Your Real Top 100

Here's a great way to put together a real list of your favorite songs (which may even include songs you didn't know were your real favorites). Go under the File menu and choose New Smart Playlist. When the dialog appears, from the first pop-up menu choose Play Count; from the second menu choose Is Greater Than; and in the text field enter "20." Then turn on the Limit To checkbox, enter "100," and choose Items. Now click OK and a new Smart Playlist will appear with only your most frequently played songs—your real top 100.

---

iTip: Making a Smart Playlist Regular

Have you fallen in love with the current content of one of your Smart Playlists? Then have iTunes make a regular playlist from your Smart Playlist (that way, it doesn't auto-update anymore). Here's how: Just click-and-drag your Smart Playlist up to the word "Playlists." The entire Playlists area will highlight and when you release your mouse button, a new regular playlist will be created with the contents of your Smart Playlist.

Smart Playlist Idea: Your Best Albums

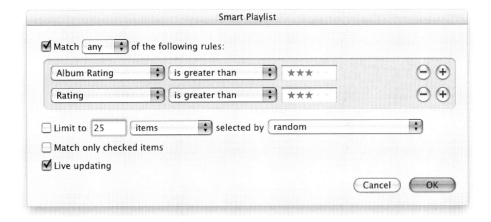

I mentioned earlier in this chapter (in an iTip on the bottom of a page) that you can turn on a feature that displays the average rating for an album (or lets you rate entire albums at once if you like). Well, you can use this feature to create a pretty slick Smart Playlist of just your top-rated songs from albums with an average rating of four stars or higher. This is slicker than it sounds, and here's why: entire albums that have lots of high-rated songs will be added to your Smart Playlist (because there are enough high-rated songs on that album to give it a four-star or higher average rating), but if, like most albums, there are only a few good songs on the albums, then for those albums, only those high-rated songs will be added, and not the ones you always skip over anyway. Go under the File menu and choose New Smart Playlist. When the dialog appears, from the first pop-up menu choose Album Rating; from the second pop-up menu choose Is Greater Than; and in the Rating field choose three stars. Then click the + (plus sign) button to add another line of criteria. From the first pop-up menu choose Rating; from the second pop-up menu choose Is Greater Than; and in the Rating field choose three stars. Here's the key thing: from the Match pop-up menu at the top of the dialog, choose Any, then click OK to create a playlist of the best songs on all your albums (and nuthin' else).

Smart Playlist Idea: Ones You Haven't Heard in a While

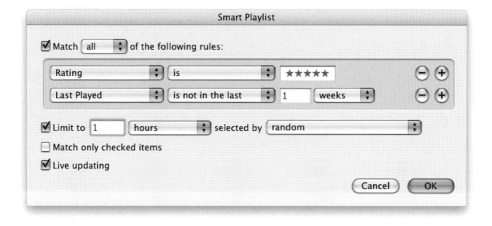

Here's how to create a one-hour-long playlist of the best songs you haven't heard in the past week, and best of all it's constantly, and automatically, updated. Go under the File menu and choose New Smart Playlist. When the dialog appears, from the first pop-up menu choose Rating; from the second pop-up menu choose Is; and in the Rating field choose five Stars. Add another line of criteria, then from the first pop-up menu choose Last Played; from the second pop-up menu choose Is Not in the Last; in the text field enter "1" and choose Weeks from the pop-up menu. Then turn on the Limit To check-box, enter "1" in the text field, and from the pop-up menu choose Hours. Then make sure the Selected By pop-up menu is set to Random. Click OK and now you'll only hear your very best songs that you haven't heard in the last week.

Chapter Twelve
Tip Drill
Cool iTunes Tips

▶▶ You'd think "Tip Drill" for a chapter about iTunes tips is just about as perfect a name as you can come up with. It totally makes sense, plus it's the name of a song from Nelly, and it's the name of a DVD documentary (which features—and was inspired by—the Nelly song of the same name). Now, being the NFL football fan that I am (Go Bucs!), when I hear "tip drill," I think of a practice drill in which a passed ball gets "tipped" by a member of the defense, making that ball much easier to intercept. NFL teams practice these tip drills all the time, and that's why in a real game, when a pass gets tipped, everybody holds their breath, because it's probably going to be intercepted. So, when I came across a song named "Tip Drill," I was drawn to it. Now, at this point it's not available from the iTunes Store, and that's probably a good thing because when I searched on the Web for the lyrics, I learned that "Tip Drill" is a very naughty song. In fact, it's mega-naughty. If my 11-year-old ever heard this song, there wouldn't be enough soap in the world to clear out the naughty passing through his ears. If it were available from the iTunes Store, I'm not sure the Explicit warning would be strong enough. It might just have to say "Yikes!" Or "Whoa, Nelly!" (Sorry, that was lame.) So, I searched for the DVD, which (not surprisingly) is about somewhat naughty things. So, to ensure that this chapter doesn't get an NC-17 rating, let's bend our song-or-movie-title-chapter-name rule and use the NFL's definition of "tip drill" instead. Thanks for understanding.

Adding Smooth Transitions Between Songs

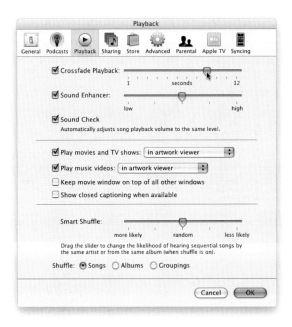

Rather than a blank gap after each song, how would you like it if when the song got near the end, it started fading out and the next song started fading in, just like they often do on the radio? iTunes can do this automatically—it's called "crossfading." You can add crossfading by going to the iTunes Preferences (under the iTunes menu on the Mac; under the Edit menu on a Windows PC) and clicking on the Playback icon. Next, turn on the checkbox for Crossfade Playback, and you're set. If you want a faster (or slower) crossfade between songs, you can adjust that using the Crossfade slider. The crossfades are measured in seconds, so for longer crossfades, drag the slider to the right. For shorter ones, drag to the left.

---

iTip: Turn Off the Arrows

When you're clicking on songs in your iTunes Music Library, you'll see lots of little right-facing arrows. These are actually shortcuts that lead you to more music from the same artist. Click on an arrow, and the iTunes Store will launch. These arrows can be very handy or very annoying, depending on your personal tolerance for little gray circles. If they're getting on your nerves, turn them off by going to iTunes' Preferences, clicking on the General icon, and then turning off Show Links to the iTunes Store. That's it—the little gray circles disappear.

Finding Your Original Songs (for Easy Backup)

Backing up your songs is important just in case anything ever happens to your hard disk, but if you haven't consolidated all your songs into the iTunes folder (as shown in Chapter 9), finding all your original songs to back up might be quite a chore. Well, here's something that can make your life a little easier. To find the original song's location on your hard disk, just Control-click (PC: Right-click) on the song in your playlist or Music Library, then from the pop-up menu that appears, choose Show in Finder on your Mac or Show in Windows Explorer on your PC. The folder where the song is located will appear in the foreground, making it easy to copy to a backup disk.

---

iTip: Changing the Font Size

The default size for type in iTunes is fairly small, and that's cool if you're 15, but if you're older (like 18 or 19), you might want the font size a bit bigger. You can do that by going to iTunes' Preferences (on the Mac, it's under the iTunes menu; on a Windows PC, it's under the Edit menu) and clicking on the General icon. You'll see pop-up menus at the top of the dialog for Source Text (the menus and such) and Song Text (the text you see in your playlists and Library). Choose Large from the pop-up menu to make the font size larger.

Editing a Song's Start/End Points

Being able to choose when a song starts (or ends) is more important than you might think. For example, the song "Baby Got Back" by Sir Mix-A-Lot starts with two Valley girls dissing some other girl's butt. It's kind of funny the first time you hear it, but by the 10th or 11th time, it really gets old. Luckily, iTunes lets you skip this part entirely by setting the Start Time for the song. Here's how: First, you need to find out exactly where in the song the "good part" starts, so play the song from the beginning and note the elapsed time when the music actually starts (in "Baby Got Back" the actual music starts 17 seconds in—the girls keep talking for a few seconds, but at least the music is playing). Now, in your Music Library (or playlist), Control-click (PC: Right-click) on the song you want to edit and choose Get Info from the contextual menu that appears. Click on the Options tab and you'll see checkboxes for Start Time and Stop Time. Click the Start Time checkbox, and then enter 0:17. That's it. Now when this song plays, it will skip over the Valley girls and get right to the music.

---

iTip: Editing the Next Song's Info

Here are two little buttons that a lot of people miss in the Get Info dialog—the Next and Previous buttons. What they do is let you, without closing this dialog, edit the next (or previous) song in the current playlist or Music Library. Just click on the Next button, and the next song's info appears in this dialog, ready to edit. I know, this may not seem like the biggest deal right now, but try it a few times and you'll be surprised at how much time you'll save.

Using Album Art to Help You Navigate

By now you've noticed that when you click on a song in iTunes, that song's album art shows in the lower left-hand corner of the iTunes window (well, at least it does if you have clicked on the Show Artwork button in the bottom-left corner of the window—it's the fourth button in the group of four). In fact, if you look directly above the album art, you'll see the words "Selected Item," which means you're seeing the art for the currently selected song. But do you know that you can change the feature so that, instead of the album showing each time you click on a song, iTunes will show the cover for the song that's now playing? That's right—just click right above the album art, directly on the words "Selected Item" and they change to "Now Playing." So, as you click on other songs, iTunes will always show you the cover for the song that's playing right now. Slick.

---

iTip: Add Cover Art to Multiple Songs

If you have an album cover that you want to apply to several songs from the same album (or a whole CD worth of songs), just Command-click (PC: Ctrl-click) on all the songs you want to apply the album art to, then Control-click (PC: Right-click) on any song and from the contextual menu that appears, choose Get Info. Now, drag-and-drop some album art into the Artwork box, and that art will be applied to all your selected songs.

Deleting Album Art

If you have album art along with one of your songs, and you decide you want to delete that art, Control-click (PC: Right-click) on the song, and from the contextual menu that appears choose Get Info. When the dialog appears, click on the Artwork tab at the top, then click on your artwork in the preview window and the Delete button below it will activate. Click that, and it's gone!

Printing Your Own CD Jewel Case Inserts

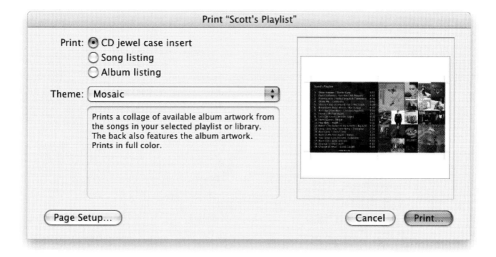

If you've burned one of your playlists to CD, you can also have iTunes print out a CD jewel case insert for you, making it easy to keep track of what's on each CD you've burned. Start by choosing which playlist you just burned to CD by clicking on it in the Source list on the left side of the iTunes dialog. Then go under the File menu and choose Print. When the Print dialog appears, click on Print: CD Jewel Case Insert (if it's not already selected). iTunes will automatically compile a list of the songs in that playlist, along with their running times, and you even have a pop-up menu in which you can choose from a selection of professional-looking "themes" for your insert, in-cluding ones that include either multiple or single album covers (you'll see a preview of each right from within the Print dialog). Once you choose your theme, just click the Print button, choose your paper size or printer in the resulting dialog, and wait for your way-cool jewel case insert to spit out of the printer.

Printing Song and Album Listings

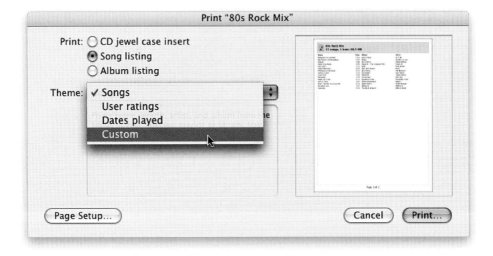

Besides printing CD jewel case inserts, iTunes also enables you to print complete lists of songs, albums, or your entire iTunes Music Library (these are great to have on hand in case your computer is ever lost, stolen, or just dies a horrible grisly death). Besides just printing simple lists, you also have control over how much information is displayed on these lists. For simple playlists, you can decide if you want title, artist, album name, running time, etc., or you can ask for a layout that includes your personal ratings. You can have the list include the last date you played each song, or you can get a complete print-out of the iTunes window view—it's all up to you (you just make your choice from the Theme pop-up menu that appears when you choose Print from the File menu, and then click on the Song Listing radio button). If you want a printout of all your albums, click on the Album Listing button instead, and you'll get both the album cover (if your songs have one), and a listing of which songs from that album appear in your playlist.

The Ultimate Space Saver

Mini Player on a Mac

Mini Player on a Windows PC

Once you start listening to a playlist in iTunes, there's no need to see all the tracks, the other playlists you're not playing, your Music Library, and basically all that other "space-stealing" stuff. To have the ultimate space-saving version of iTunes (called the iTunes Mini Player), just click once on the green + (plus sign) button in the upper-left corner of the iTunes window (on a Mac), which shrinks iTunes into the Mini Player. If you're on a Windows PC, choose Switch to Mini Player from the Advanced menu (or press Ctrl-M) to get to the Mini Player. Best of all, you still have access to the most important controls— Play, Rewind, Fast Forward, Volume, and Eject. To return to full size, just click the green button again (for the Mac) or click on the Maximize/Restore button (for Windows).

---

iTip: Keep Mini Player on Top

If you're using the iTunes Mini Player, it's so small that you can have it always appear in front of your other open applications (so your controls are always right there where you need them, in case the boss walks in). Just go to the iTunes Preferences (under the iTunes menu on the Mac; under the Edit menu on a Windows PC), then click on the Advanced icon. Click on the General tab, then turn on the checkbox for Keep Mini Player on Top of All Other Windows, and then click OK. Now, you can control iTunes without leaving your open applications.

Converting Your Songs

Here's a little-known tip for converting your imported songs to WAV format (so they can play on virtually any CD player). You start by going to iTunes' Preferences (on the Mac, under the iTunes menu; on a Windows PC, under the Edit menu), clicking on the Advanced icon and choosing Importing. Then, from the Import Using pop-up menu, choose WAV Encoder. Next, go to your playlist (or Music Library), hold the Command key (PC: Ctrl key) and click on the songs you want to convert to WAV. Once they're all selected, just Control-click (PC: Right-click) on any of the selected songs and from the contextual menu that appears, choose Convert Selection to WAV. The converted versions of your songs will appear directly below each original MP3 or M4A version in your Music Library. By the way, if you want to save these WAV files to a different folder on your hard disk, just press-and-hold the Option key (PC: Shift key) before you choose Convert Selection to WAV from the contextual menu. This doesn't work on songs that are in the protected AAC format (like songs from the ITS).

---

iTip: How to Shuffle Albums

Did you know that you can set iTunes to shuffle albums randomly? So iTunes will shuffle just the albums themselves—NOT the songs on the albums. If you want to turn this feature on, just go to the iTunes Preferences (under the iTunes menu on the Mac; under the Edit menu on a Windows PC) and click on the Playback icon. Then under Smart Shuffle, choose Albums instead of Songs, and then click OK.

Moving Playlists Between Computers

If you have more than one computer (let's say you have a desktop machine and a laptop), you probably want access to your iTunes playlists on both machines, right? Well, you could set up a wireless network, blah, blah, blah, or you could simply export your playlist from your desktop machine, and then import that playlist in iTunes on your laptop. Here's how: Just Control-click (PC: Right-click) on the playlist you want to export, then choose Export Song List from the contextual menu that appears. Now, save it and transfer that playlist (text file) to your other computer (put it on a USB drive, burn it to CD, email it to yourself, whatever), then go under the iTunes File menu and choose Import. Locate that exported playlist file and click Choose or Open—that playlist is now in your laptop's iTunes. Ahhh, but there's a catch (you knew it couldn't be that easy, right?). What you've imported is a "list" of songs—not the songs themselves. If the songs don't already appear in the iTunes Music Library on the "other" computer, you may need to transfer the actual MP3 and AAC song files (again, you can burn them to CD or use your iPod as a hard drive [see Chapter 4 on how to do that]). Once the songs are copied onto your laptop (and placed in your iTunes Music folder), you can then use your imported playlist to hear those songs.

Sharing Your Music over a Network

If you're connected to a network (at home, at the office, at school, etc.), you can let other people on the network listen to any (or all) of your iTunes playlists. That's right, you can reveal your own highly refined musical taste by letting other people spend some time in "your world." Best of all, setting it up takes about five seconds. First go to the iTunes Preferences (under the iTunes menu on the Mac; under the Edit menu on a Windows PC) and click on the Sharing icon. Then turn on the checkbox for Share My Library on My Local Network. That's it. By default, iTunes wants you to share all your music, but if you'd prefer not to share all of your playlists, then click on the Share Selected Playlists button, and from the scrolling list choose which playlists you want to be shared—just click in the empty box to put a checkmark by any one you want to share. Click OK and you're sharing. Now, when other people on the network launch iTunes, they'll see a new listing in their Source list called "Shared," and under that link will be a list of people (yourself included) who are making their playlists available. They can click on your playlist, see your songs, and decide which ones they want to listen to, just as if the songs were on their own drive (but don't worry—they can't copy your songs to either their hard disk or iPod—they're just for listening only while you're sharing). (*Note:* To see their shared music, click on the Look for Shared Libraries checkbox in the dialog.) When you log off the network, your playlists go with you. If you only want certain people (cool people, no doubt) to be able to hear your shared lists, click the Require Password checkbox and enter a password. Then only the people you tell the password to will be allowed into your special world. What a great opportunity for you to be elitist.

iTunes Radio Is on the Air!

Throughout this book we've been pretty much treating iTunes as a way to organize and play your imported CDs and downloaded songs; but if you've got an Internet connection, there's another side to iTunes that they don't talk about at parties, and that's iTunes Radio. Well, it's not exactly FM radio, but instead it's a list of hundreds of streaming Internet radio stations, covering 20 different genres, broadcasting everything from reggae to talk shows, from metal to classical (and everything in between). The reason many people don't know about this cool hidden feature is that it's likely hidden from view in the Source list. To see the current list of stations, go to the iTunes Preferences (on the Mac, it's under the iTunes menu; on a Windows PC, it's under the Edit menu) and click on the General icon. Then, under the Show section (near the top of the dialog), turn on the checkbox for Radio. Now a Radio link will appear in your Source list. Click on it to see the list of radio genres. To see the stations currently broadcasting for a particular genre, double-click the genre's name. To listen to a station, just double-click the station's name in the list.

Making Playlists of Your Favorite Stations

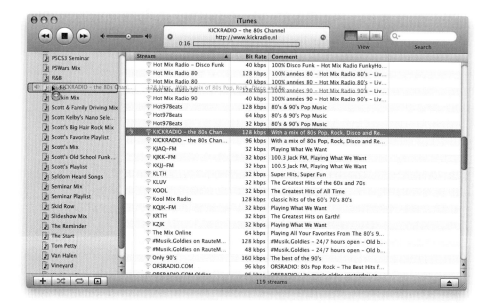

In your local FM market, there are a limited number of stations, and out of those there are probably only six or seven that you listen to often (and are programmed into the presets on your car stereo), but with iTunes streaming Internet radio, there are hundreds of stations. Even though there are hundreds, you'll still wind up picking out your favorites; it's just that you might have 28 favorites instead of only six or seven. Luckily, keeping track of your favorites is pretty easy—just put them into a playlist as if they were songs. Start by clicking the Create a Playlist button in the bottom-left corner of the iTunes window, name your playlist "Radio," then click on the Radio link in the Source list. Find the stations you like, and drag-and-drop them right onto your Radio playlist. Now the next time you want to hear them, just click on the playlist, then double-click on your favorite station to start the streaming.

---

iTip: Streaming Radio Song Info

Similar to satellite radio, many of these streaming Internet radio stations also broadcast the name and artist for the songs they play. To see the name and artist for the current song, look up in the iTunes status display. By the way, since you can log in to a station at any point in the song, the elapsed time you see displayed in the iTunes status display isn't the elapsed time for the song; it's a running count of how long you've been listening to that particular station, which could help you determine if you need to seek psychological help for a streaming-radio addiction problem.

It's Time to Get Visual

If you ever wanted a glimpse of what your parents' lives were like back when they were in their 20s, just press Command-T (PC: Ctrl-T), which turns on iTunes' visual effects (called the Visualizer). So why did Apple include these "way out" (a '60s term) visuals in iTunes? So your parents could relate to them and feel good about buying you a computer and an iPod (hey, it's possible). Anyway, the images created by the Visualizer are actually pretty cool because they react to the music you're playing in iTunes, and just watching them gives you the munchies (did I say that out loud?). *Warning:* Whatever you do, don't buy the single "Are You Experienced?" by Jimi Hendrix (from the iTunes Store) and have it playing while running the Visualizer as your parents are walking by your screen. They'll totally freak (and may quit their jobs).

---

iTip: Full–Screen Visualizing

Normally, the Visualizer "does its thing" by taking over your iTunes window, but we need to experience the entire trip in its full–screen splendor. So start the Visualizer (see above), press Command-F (PC: Ctrl-F), and then sit back and stare directly into the screen. Enter into a hypnotic trance, then you can call in sick for work: "Sorry man, I can't come in today. I'm hypnotized." By the way, to end your full–screen "trance," press the Esc key on your keyboard. To switch back from Full Screen to containing the Visualizer within the iTunes window, press Command-F again.

Maximize Your Experience

If you have a fast computer, the Visualizer runs very quickly, with no jerkiness, stuttering, or other distractions. But if you're running iTunes on a computer that has a few miles on it, you might need to tweak the visuals a bit so they perform at their psychedelic best on your machine (after all, having smooth visuals is key to helping you achieve harmony of mind, body, and spirit—or some crap like that). That's why you need access to the Visualizer's options. When the Visualizer is "visualizing" within the iTunes window (not Full Screen mode), go to the View menu, under Visualizer, and choose Options. The Visualizer Options dialog will appear, in which you can display and/or slow down the frame rate and choose a faster (but rougher) onscreen display.

---

iTip: Visualize the Apple Logo

Okay, let's say you're sitting around trippin' on the visuals, and some friends come over. Have them stare directly into the center of the screen, tell them to focus their inner "chi" on that spot, and before long the spiritual epicenter of all that is cool will be revealed to them. Then, while they're focusing their inner chi, slowly move your hand over the keyboard and press the letter B, which makes the Apple logo fade into view, right in the center of the visuals, revealing the source of all that's cool. This is what's known in high-tech marketing jargon as "optimum logo placement." (Note: This feature may vary depending on your version of iTunes.)

Controlling the Visuals

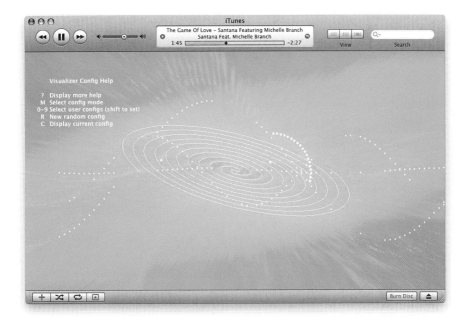

If you think the Visualizer is just a random set of visual randomness that's totally random, well, my friend, I have a startling revelation for you—it only "kind of" is. That's because you actually can control some aspects of the Visualizer while it's...well...visualizing. There are different one-key commands you can give while it's running to make it bend to your every whim. So what are these one-key wonders? While it's running, press the Question Mark (?) key and a list of basic commands will appear in the upper left-hand corner. Press the Question Mark key again for another list of options. To select an option, press the corresponding key on your keyboard.

---

iTip: Displaying Song Info

When the Visualizer is running and a new song starts, the song's name, artist, album art (if present), and album name appear for a few moments in the bottom left-hand corner of the screen, then they slowly fade away (so as not to distract from the mind-bending array of patterns that will soon take over your screen, and perhaps even your life). However, if you'd like the song info not to fade away—to always be displayed—just go under the View menu, under Visualizer, and choose Options—to bring up the Visualizer Options dialog. Now just turn on the checkbox for Always Display Song Info. Plus, if the song you're playing has accompanying album art, it's displayed, too.

Extreme Visuals

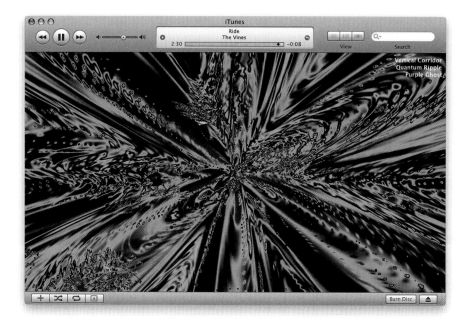

Here's the problem with visuals: There'll come a time when you're not getting a visual buzz anymore, and you need something stronger. So you press the letter Z and something cool happens. And that keeps you happy—for a while. But then you press it again, and again, and each time you press it, it gives you a different set of colors, and pretty soon you're pressing Z over and over again (notice the different configurations listed in the top-right corner of the iTunes window). But then that's not enough, and you press Q and your visuals just freak. But after a while, that just doesn't do it for you, and then eventually some friends talk you into trying the letter A, and I can't quite explain what pressing A does, but it's a stronger effect than Z or Q, and a lot of people get really strung out on A. That's the problem with the Visualizer. It's hard to stay just a casual user. You just keep pressing all the letters on your keyboard until you start to freak out.

---

iTip: Third–Party Visualizers

After a while, pressing Z, Q, and even A—it's kid stuff, and you go looking for something more. You'll probably wind up on a website like soundspectrum.com, downloading third–party Visualizer plug-ins. Install the plug-ins by putting them in iTunes' Plug-ins folder (on the Mac, look inside your Home folder, in the Library, in the iTunes folder, and there you'll find the iTunes Plug-ins folder; on a Windows PC: in the Program Files folder, inside the iTunes folder, create a "Plug-ins" folder). Once you've installed them, go under iTunes' Visualizer menu and you'll see your plug-ins appear at the bottom of the menu.

Balancing the Volume Between Songs

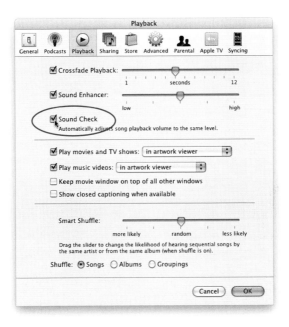

One of the perils of having an eclectic taste in music is that all music isn't recorded at the same volume. For example, if the first song in one of your playlists is "Concerto for Piano No. 21 in C Major, K 467, 2nd Movement, Andante," and the next song following that happens to be "I'm a Dog" by Kid Rock, I have to tell you that when "I'm a Dog" comes on, the volume (and sheer mass) of that song will send you scrambling for the Volume slider. If there were only some way that piano concertos and rock-rap could share the same volume setting. Ah, but there is: it's called Sound Check, and this iTunes preference setting lets you automatically balance the volume between songs just like your iPod does. Just go to the iTunes Preferences (found under the iTunes menu on a Mac, or the Edit menu on a PC), and then click on the Playback icon. Next, turn on the checkbox beside Sound Check to turn on iTunes' automatic volume balancing. So now when you glide from Frank Sinatra straight into Metallica, it'll be a smooth transition (at least, volumewise).

---

iTip: Keyboard Volume Adjustment

If you want to change the volume while you're playing a song, you don't have to grab the mouse and travel all the way up to the top-left corner—instead you can adjust the volume right from your keyboard. To "crank up the jams," press Command-Up Arrow (PC: Ctrl-Up Arrow) and to turn it back down (when the cops arrive), press Command-Down Arrow (PC: Ctrl-Down Arrow).

Making Your Music Sound Better

By default, the iTunes graphic equalizer (EQ) is set to flat, which is basically the same as setting the bass and treble sliders on your car stereo to the zero setting (flat is actually a good name for this state, because that's how it makes your stereo sound—flat). But you can use iTunes' built-in EQ to make your music sound dramatically better, and you don't have to understand how EQs work—presets based on the type of music you listen to are already built-in. Here's how to turn on iTunes' EQ: Go under the View menu and choose Show Equalizer. At the top of the Equalizer dialog is a pop-up menu with presets—just choose the type of music you're listening to, and iTunes creates an EQ setting to make your music sound its best. If you want to create your own setting, just grab the sliders (bass on the left, midrange in the middle, and highs on the right), and make your own.

---

iTip: Creating Custom EQ Presets

If you've created your own custom EQ setting (I created one for my laptop by starting with the R&B preset and then tweaking the Bass sliders), you can save it as your own custom preset. Once you've got your EQ set the way you want it, choose Make Preset from the presets pop-up menu in the Equalizer dialog. Name your preset in the resulting dialog. When you click OK, your preset is added to the presets pop-up menu and will appear in alphabetical order.

Individual EQ Settings by Song

I know what you're thinking: "Okay Scott, I set my overall EQ for iTunes to Rock, but some of my songs are R&B, some are classical, and some are dance. So my rock songs will sound great, but the rest are going to be EQ'd for rock, so they won't sound their best, right?" Right. That's why iTunes lets you assign EQs to individual songs, so you can assign an R&B EQ to R&B songs, and a Classical EQ to classical pieces. Here's how: Press Command-J (PC: Ctrl-J) to bring up the View Options, then turn on the checkbox beside Equalizer and an Equalizer column will appear in your iTunes window. To assign an EQ to a song, click on the song, then choose the EQ you want for that song from the EQ column's pop-up menu.

---

iTip: Setting the EQ for Multiple Songs

Applying EQ settings on a song-by-song basis can take some time, so here's a big timesaving shortcut: First, click on the Genre column to sort your songs by genre, then Shift-click the first song and the last song to select all the songs in that genre. Now Control-click (PC: Right-click) on any selected song, and in the contextual menu choose Get Info to bring up the Multiple Item Information dialog. Under the Equalizer Preset pop-up menu, choose an EQ preset and then click OK.

How Many Playlists Does a Song Appear In?

If you seem to be hearing a particular song an awful lot, it may be that the song appears in several different playlists, so you wind up changing playlists but still hearing that song again. Luckily, there's a slick way to find out exactly how many (and which) playlists a particular song appears in—just Control-click (PC: Right-click) on a song, and from the contextual menu that appears, go under Show in Playlist to see a list of the playlists that contain that song. If you see quite a long list, you'll know why you've been hearing it so much.

---

iTip: Finding Duplicates

Because you'll wind up having hundreds, maybe thousands, of songs in iTunes, and lots of different playlists, you'll be amazed at how easy it is to have more than one copy of a song (maybe with a slightly different name, or just in different playlists, or different versions of the same song). Luckily, there's a quick way to get rid of the duplicates—just go under the View menu and choose Show Duplicates. This will bring up a list of all your duplicate songs. Then, if you have two (or more) copies, you can quickly click on the one(s) you want to delete and press the Delete (PC: Backspace) key on your keyboard.

Viewing Your Playlists with Album Art

Besides Cover Flow (see the next page), there is another visual way to view the music in your playlists, and that is the Grouped Artwork View. This view features large album covers on the left side of your main window, with the info about each song appearing on the right side. To get to this view, simply click the center View button at the top-right side of the iTunes window (circled in red above). You can still sort by different criteria by clicking on Name, or Artist, or Genre, or any column header.

Browse Your Playlist with Cover Flow

Cover Flow is the most visual (and certainly coolest) way to browse through your iTunes Music Library (or any playlist), because it's kind of like browsing through an actual CD collection in your home or at the local record store. To enter Cover Flow view, click the third View icon from the left (at the top right of the iTunes window, shown circled above) and the covers appear above your list view. You can browse through your covers in any of these three ways: (1) drag the scrubber bar directly below the covers, (2) use the Left and Right Arrow keys on your keyboard, or (3) just click on any album cover you see, even if it's partially covered, and it comes to the front. When you stop on a cover, the song info is displayed in the list that appears directly below the Cover Flow view. To hear the song, either double-click on the album art itself, or on the highlighted song in the list. Also, while you're in this Cover Flow view, you can choose different sorting methods (by Name, by Genre, by My Rating, etc.) just like you would in a regular playlist view by clicking on the column headers in the list below the Cover Flow view, and the covers are then displayed in that order. Wicked cool, eh?

---

iTip: Jump to the Right Song

In Cover Flow view, if you know the name of the song you want and the Name category is highlighted in your list view, you can just type the first few letters of the song name and iTunes will jump to the first song in your playlist that begins with those letters. This also works for Artist and Album when those categories are highlighted.

Chapter Thirteen
Add It On
iPod Accessories

The Bruces' song "Add It On" got the honor of being the name for this chapter about iPod accessories. Okay, granted, I'm not sure if it's exactly an "honor" being chosen for a chapter name here, but it certainly beats getting nominated for a Grammy and then losing to Nelly (even though that never happened to "Add It On," but hey, it could've). Actually, now that you mention it, I wouldn't mind coming up with my own music award. Instead of a "Grammy" I could call it a "Scotty," and the award itself would either look like a small Scottish dog, or it could resemble James Doohan, who played Chief Engineer Montgomery "Scotty" Scott in the original Star Trek series. Now, if it were up to my friend Terry White, he'd definitely name it a "Scotty" because he's a big Star Trek freak. There's a difference between a Star Trek freak and a Star Trek geek. You see, although Terry knows all the characters, plots, equipment, etc., by name and has even attended the occasional Star Trek convention, he claims he doesn't "dress up in costume" when he goes to the convention. He says that's "crossing the line." Yeah, I'm sure that's where the line is (wink, wink). I digress. Anyway, this chapter is about all the cool things you can add to your already cool iPod to make it so cool that it loses all its original coolness. Cool!

Bose SoundDock Portable

If your goal is to get the best possible sound quality from a "designed-for-the-iPod" desk-top speaker system, then you've got to check out the new Bose SoundDock Portable. This builds on Bose's classic SoundDock (which I featured in previous editions of this book) by offering even better sound, a new auxiliary input that lets you play other audio devices through the system (like a cassette player, a CD player, or even your computer), and it looks more streamlined because the dock actually retracts out of the way when not in use. At $399, it's not cheap, but when it comes to sheer quality of sound, it's argu-ably the best in its class. It works with any iPod that has a dock connector on the bottom, plus it comes with a handy wireless remote so you can control it from across the room, and it even comes with a built-in handle, making it much more portable than the origi-nal model. You can find it at the Apple Store (online or in the mall) or at Bose.com.

JBL Radial Micro Loudspeaker Dock

If space and money are both in shorter supply, you're going to love JBL's Radial Micro Loudspeaker Dock. It's a very futuristic-looking little setup (it comes in either white or black), and your iPod looks great just sitting there in its Universal Dock—even when it's not playing—and it doesn't take up much desk space. In fact, this speaker system is so small you could easily take it on the road. Like the Bose system, it charges your iPod (even when the system isn't on, it still charges), it comes with a wireless remote, and it, too, features an Audio In jack. The sound is surprisingly good for its small size, and you can turn it up much louder than the small size would lead you to believe. The price is small, too, at around $149. You can find it at the Apple Store (online or in the mall) or at JBL.com.

iHome iH6 Dual Alarm iPod Clock Radio

PHOTO BY SCOTT KELBY

If you travel with your iPod and want a first-rate portable speaker system, or if you just want an incredibly small set of speakers at a great price, take a look at the iHome iH6 Dual Alarm Clock Radio for your iPod. It has a built-in dock and charges your iPod when docked, plus the system folds up so it's very compact for traveling. It operates with an AC Power Adapter, but since it's an alarm as well, it comes with a battery backup in case the power goes out. The iHome iH6 comes with a wireless remote, it has a built-in dual alarm (I guess you knew that from the name, eh?), which you can set to sleep at a specific time or wake you with music, and a built-in AM/FM receiver. It also has an Audio In port, so it can be used as computer speakers, as well. It sells for around $99, comes in white or black, and can be found at Apple.com, your local Apple store, or at iHomeAudio.com.

Get Wireless Control and Convenience with Apple's Universal Dock

When you bought your iPod, did you notice that in the box there was this white plastic adapter that doesn't seem to fit anywhere? Well, that's a dock adapter for use with the Apple iPod Universal Dock (sold separately), and in short—Docks rock. Your iPod sits upright in the Dock (making it easy to see your iPod's screen), and the Dock connects to your computer, so you just sit your iPod in the Dock to charge and/or sync it with your computer (this beats digging behind your computer to connect a cable every time you want to sync up). Plus, Apple now includes a wireless remote, so you can play and pause, jump to the next song, raise/lower the volume, choose different playlists— all while your iPod is docked. There's even a Line Out port on the back of the Dock, so you can connect your iPod to your TV or stereo system using the Apple iPod AV Cable (see Chapter 6 for more on that cable or an S-video cable). Anyway, the Universal Dock sells for $49, and you can get it from Apple.com or your local Apple Store.

Charging Your iPod without Your Computer

Sometimes, you just can't get to your computer to recharge your iPod (you could be on a vacation where you don't have access to your computer, or you're traveling with a laptop, or…well, you get the idea). In that case, I recommend the Apple iPod USB Power Adapter (only $29). This lets you recharge your iPod from a regular AC outlet, and it connects to your iPod using the USB cable that comes with the adapter, or you can connect it to Apple's Universal Dock and then just put your iPod into the Dock. You can find it at Apple.com or at your local Apple Store.

Add FM Radio to Your iPod

Here's a fairly brilliant accessory from Apple that adds real FM radio to your iPod. It's called the iPod Radio Remote, and the reason it's got the "Remote" added to the name is because besides adding FM to your iPod, it comes with a wired remote control that lets you control more than just the radio (which appears in the main screen of your iPod, just like movies, videos, music, etc.), it lets you control pretty much everything—from which song is playing to which video is playing. The remote plugs into the dock connector on the bottom of your iPod, and although there is a cable attached to the remote (after all, it's a "wired" remote), the remote itself weighs almost nothing. If you want FM on your iPod, this is the best $49 you'll spend. Get it from Apple.com or your local Apple Store.

Protect Your iPod from Scratches

I'm one of those people who'll toss my iPod into the same pants pocket with my car keys without a second thought, and my iPods all have the scratches to prove it. However, my tech editor Terry cringes at that scenario, and that's why he turned me on to the Power Support Crystal Film Cover, which puts a very thin, totally clear protective film layer over the Click Wheel, LCD screen, and the front and back of your iPod. You'd hardly know it's there, but it protects your iPod from nasty scratches and keeps it looking like new. Best of all, you can easily remove the film, reapply it, clean it...whatever, and it doesn't make your iPod all sticky (how do you like that technical phraseology—"all sticky"?). Another advantage of this type of super-thin clear "protective case" for your iPod is that it enables you to easily use the car adapters for your iPod, many of which won't work if you have a bulky leather or plastic case around your iPod. Apple sells this film for $15 on Apple .com, at your local Apple Store, or buy it direct from PowerSupportUSA.com.

Add a Second Skin to Your iPod

PHOTO BY SCOTT KELBY

Another popular way to protect your iPod from scratches and damage is to put it in some sort of protective case, like the Incase Neoprene Sleeve for the iPod classic. It comes with a belt clip on the back (you can also clip it to your purse, providing of course, you have a purse), and it's designed so you can access all the controls, including the dock connector, without having to remove it from the case. It's $29.95 and you can get it from Apple.com, your local Apple Store, or direct from goincase.com.

Turn Your iPod into a Nike Personal Trainer

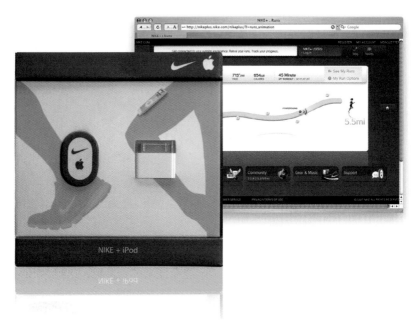

What happens when you take two companies who pretty much have the lock on the "coolness factor" (Apple and Nike), and combine their creativity into one product? You get the Nike + iPod Sports Kit, which turns your iPod nano (and Nike sneakers) into your own high-tech digital personal trainer. This kit comes with a wireless sensor that inserts into specially-designed Nike + sneakers. (Note: You don't have to use Nike + sneakers—you could technically insert the sensor into other sneakers if you can find a way to keep them in place, it's just that the Nike + have a special pocket under the insole designed to hold the sensor, so they're a natural choice.) This sensor sends information about your workout (your walk, jog, run, etc.) to a tiny receiver attached to your iPod nano and you get live feedback on your workout, including calories burned, how far you've traveled, etc. It even provides voice feedback, and will hurl insults at you if you're not moving fast enough (okay, it doesn't hurl insults, but I bet Apple would sell twice as many if it did). Now, if that isn't cool enough, when you're done with your run, you can upload your data from the run each day to a special Nike + website (shown above), where you can analyze your workout routine and see your progress charted onscreen. There are also special Nike Sport Music downloads and mixes, and custom workouts featuring tips and personal training–style coaching from a Nike coach that are available through the iTunes Store. The Nike + iPod Sports Kit is only $29 from Apple.com, Niketown, or your Nike dealer. (By the way, if you get this kit, Nike makes a special iPod nano armband holder you might like, too.)

Colorize Your iPod

The iPod classic comes in two colors: silver or black. But if you feel that you need to add some serious color to your iPod world, then the folks at ColorWare can hook you up. They specialize in two things: (1) colorizing your existing iPod, or (2) selling brand new colorized iPods (and other computer stuff) that they colorize in their labs. If you want them to colorize your existing iPod, here's how it works: You go to their website and pick a color or a color combo (you can choose to have the body, Click Wheel, and Select button be different colors, so you have a three-color iPod—it just costs a little more), and you get a preview of how your colorized iPod will look (as shown above). Then you ship them your iPod, and shortly thereafter you get back a colorized iPod (with a scratch-resistant coating) that looks like it came in color from the factory. They have 29 colors to choose from (including a cool steel finish), and prices range from $64 to around $104, depending on which version of the iPod you have, and whether you want one color, two colors, or three colors. Even if you're not longing for a color iPod, it's worth a stop by the site just to see what iPods in 29 different colors look like. They're at ColorWarePC.com. (By the way, they also colorize iPod nanos and iPod touches, as well.)

iPod nano Armbands

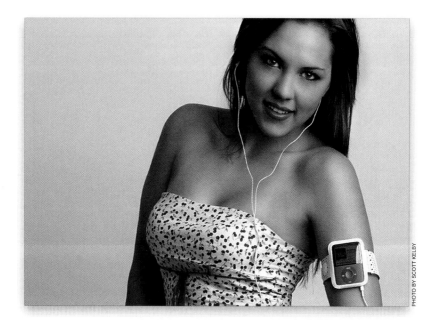

PHOTO BY SCOTT KELBY

If you want to literally wear your iPod nano when you're jogging or working out, you need an iPod nano armband. It holds your nano firmly in place and keeps it within arm's length at all times. (Get, it? Arm's length. Okay, sorry about that one.) Probably the most popular armband is Apple's own iPod nano Armband, which comes in gray (at least it only came in gray when this book was published, but if history is any indicator, more colors will be released soon), and sells for about $29 at Apple.com or your local Apple Store. Besides the Apple model, Incase offers it's neoprene Sports Armband for the iPod nano for $29.95 at goincase.com.

Note: The model shown above is *Photoshop®User TV* news anchor Stephanie Cross, who became famous around the Web from her role as "The iPod flea Girl" in the "iPod flea" parody video, which you can find on YouTube.com or one of a hundred other places on the Web. Her brother, Michael (shown on page 8), also co-starred in the video, and they're both shown here in the book wearing the same outfits they did in the video. Just for the record, I generally hate people who still fit into clothes they wore when they were much younger, but for these two great people, I'll make an exception.

Bose QuietComfort 2 and 3 Headphones

If you do a reasonable amount of air travel, you'll fall in love with the Bose QuietComfort Acoustic Noise Canceling Headphones. Besides just being great-sounding headphones (with great bass response), what makes this headphone set rock is its noise-canceling feature (which is absolutely amazing, and precisely why these work so well for air travel—they cancel out pretty much everything except the music or audio track for your videos). These headphones are almost legendary with frequent flyers, and using them with your iPod is the height of luxury, as evidenced by their price—about $299. Hey, I said they were great, I didn't say they were cheap. The Series 2 are pictured here, but Bose also came out with a Series 3, which some people love and others don't like at all (which is why, I imagine, the Series 2 are still available for sale). The Series 3 are smaller and don't cover your entire ear like the Series 2, which some people apparently like. However, here are my four beefs with the Series 3: (1) the headphones themselves are smaller, but the case they travel in isn't, so they don't save any space, (2) they use a rechargeable lithium-ion battery, which means if the battery runs out while you're flying, you can't simply pop in a new AAA battery like you could with the Series 2, (3) they cost $50 more than the Series 2, and (4) on a long flight, the Series 3 hurt my ears where the Series 2 never did. Buy hey, that's just me. You can find them at Bose.com, on Apple.com, or wherever crazy-expensive headphones are sold.

Bose In-Ear Headphones

If you just want an outstanding pair of headphones and noise canceling isn't a concern for you (you're not using them on flights or subway commutes), then check out Bose's In-Ear headphones. They're lightweight, the sound quality is superb for this style of in-ear headphone (with surprisingly good bass response), they come with a nice carrying case, and they're much less expensive (at only $99.95) than either the Bose QuiteComfort second- or third-generation headphones. You can find them at Apple's online store or check them out at Bose.com.

The Next Step Up from the Free Earbuds

if you don't want to spend a lot of dough, but you want better-sounding audio than you get from the free earbuds that come with your iPod, check out Apple's iPod In-Ear Headphones. Although they're not technically "noise-cancelling" headphones, because of the shape of the ear caps, they do block out some of the ambient background noise, along with giving you better-quality sound all around. They're $39 and you can get them from Apple (either the online store, or the one at the mall).

AirPort Express for Streaming iTunes

Apple's AirPort Express Base Station with AirTunes keeps on racking up national awards for its brilliant design as a wireless network device. But what you want it for is AirTunes, which gives you the ability to transmit your iTunes music wirelessly to your stereo (or just a pair of powered speakers) anywhere in your house, your office, hotel room—you name it. Think about it: your computer is in one room, but you're hearing your iTunes playlists on a stereo in another room of your house, and it's all wireless. Plus, the setup is a no-brainer, and the whole thing works astonishingly well. You can buy it direct from Apple for around $99, and it's worth every penny!

---

iTip: Controlling iTunes

Once iTunes is playing, if you want to skip a song, repeat a song, pause a song, etc., you can do all of that without having to actually go into iTunes. That's because you can access these basic controls directly from the Dock (on a Mac) or the Taskbar (on a PC). On the Mac, just Control-click (or click-and-hold) on the iTunes icon in the Dock and a contextual menu of commands will appear. On a Windows PC, Right-click the iTunes icon in the Taskbar's Navigation Area and a similar pop-up menu will appear.

Chapter Fourteen

Lido Shuffle

How to Use Apple's iPod shuffle

When I heard Apple chose to name their flash-memory-based iPod the "iPod shuffle," I was thrilled—mostly because it made my job of coming up with a song-based title for this chapter much easier. Two songs immediately came to mind: I could've gone with Queen's "Flash," and in most any situation going with a Queen song is a safe bet, as they're rather revered in the rock music world. However, the song "Flash" sucks. I'm sorry, but it does. You know it does. I know it does. If I played the song for my 11-year-old son (who thankfully doesn't use the word "sucks"), even he would find himself with no other choice but to use the word "sucks" as well, and I don't want to put him in that awkward position. So instead, I went with "Lido Shuffle," which is one of Boz Skaggs' coolest songs. Now, both of these songs are from the '80s, which automatically means they come with a measure of suckiness built right in, but we're simply going to overlook that, because it makes my job of naming the chapter even easier, and really, that's what this is all about: making my life easy. Hey, speaking of easy (how's that for a lame segue?), the iPod shuffle is fairly easy, thanks to the fact that it has no screen. When I first learned it had no screen, rather than calling it the iPod shuffle, I thought Apple should've named it something like iPod Blind or iPod in the Dark. Sadly, Apple never called me for my opinion. Or, I would've told them to name it iPod Bad Queen Song. That's probably why Apple didn't call.

Getting Songs onto Your iPod shuffle

Getting songs onto your iPod shuffle couldn't be easier—you simply place your iPod shuffle onto the Dock that comes with it, and connect the Dock to the USB port on your computer (by the way, the little plug on the Dock connects to the headphone jack on your iPod shuffle). The first time you do this, iTunes will automatically launch and a dialog will appear asking you to name your iPod shuffle. Then, iTunes will automatically choose exactly enough songs from your Music Library to fill your iPod shuffle with a random selection of songs (just in case you were wondering, it fills your iPod shuffle with about 240 songs. Of course, provided you have at least 240 songs in your Music Library). This automatic filling of your iPod shuffle is called (no big surprise here) the Autofill feature.

---

iTip: Deleting a Song

To delete a song from your iPod shuffle, just click on the iPod shuffle icon that appears in the iTunes Source list (on the left side of the iTunes window) when your iPod shuffle is connected to your computer. When you do this, all the songs on your iPod shuffle will appear in the main window. To delete a song, just click on it and press the Delete (PC: Backspace) key on your keyboard.

Getting Songs You Actually Want

The first time you plug your iPod shuffle into your computer, iTunes just picks random songs from your Music Library and downloads those into your iPod shuffle until it's full. However, rather than using your full Music Library, you probably will want to have it choose songs from one of your playlists instead. (For example, when iTunes first down-loaded songs into my iPod shuffle, it also took along some Christmas songs. That'd be fine in December, but sadly, it was September.) So, to have iTunes autofill from a playlist (rather than from your entire Music Library), just connect your iPod shuffle, then click on your iPod shuffle's icon in the Source list on the left side of the iTunes window. Then click on the Contents tab in the top center of the screen to reveal the contents of your iPod, and the Autofill panel will appear just below your main iTunes window (shown above). In the Autofill From pop-up menu, choose the playlist you want Autofill to pull songs from, and then click on the Autofill button on the left side of the panel. As long as you have the Replace All Items When Autofilling checkbox turned on, iTunes will delete the songs that were on your iPod shuffle when you first plugged it in (if there actually were any songs there) and replace them with songs from your currently selected playlist.

Turning On Your iPod shuffle

The switch for turning on the iPod shuffle is on the bottom. To turn the iPod on, slide the round button to the right (as shown above), revealing a green bar. Also, when you turn the iPod shuffle on, a green LED status light appears for just a few seconds, to the right of the On/Off button. To turn your iPod shuffle off, just slide the button back over to the left, to the OFF position (covering the green bar).

---

iTip: Get a Better Random Playlist

Want Autofill to show a bit more discretion when choosing songs for your iPod shuffle? Then make sure you turn on the Autofill radio button for Choose Higher Rated Items More Often. That way, when it randomly grabs the 240 or so songs, it'll make sure that songs you've rated higher (the songs you like best) get chosen more often than the rest. So basically, you get a better random playlist.

Hearing the Songs on Your iPod shuffle

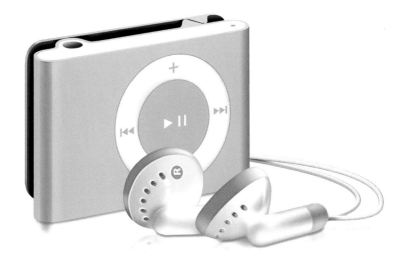

All right, your songs are on your iPod shuffle—now it's time to hear them. Plug the ear-buds (which come with your iPod shuffle) into the headphone jack on the top of the iPod shuffle, and then press the Play/Pause button in the center of the circular Control Pad to hear a song. To pause (stop) the currently playing song, just press the center Play/Pause button again. If you don't like the currently playing song, you can skip past it by pressing the Next/Fast-Forward button on the right side of the circular Control Pad (needless to say, if you press the left button, it plays the previous song—that's why it's called the Previous/Rewind button). By the way, if you press-and-hold the Next/Fast-Forward button (rather than just pressing it once), the iPod shuffle fast forwards through the currently playing song (and of course, holding down the Previous/Rewind button rewinds the song).

---

iTip: Jump to the Beginning

If at any time you want to jump back to the beginning of your playlist, just press the Play/Pause button three times really fast.

Adjusting the Volume

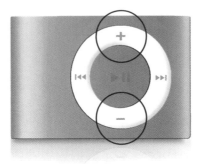

To turn the volume up, press the Plus (+) button on the top of the circular Control Pad. To lower the volume, press the Minus (–) button at the bottom of the pad.

---

iTip: Listen to Audiobooks

If you want to listen to audiobooks with your iPod shuffle—no problem, you just have to drag them over into your iPod shuffle manually, because the iTunes Autofill feature doesn't include audiobooks. It's weird that way. Always has been.

Manually Adding Songs to Your iPod shuffle

You don't have to use Autofill to get songs onto your iPod shuffle—just drag-and-drop the songs that you want from your iTunes Music Library directly onto the iPod shuffle icon that appears in the Source list (on the left side of the iTunes window) when your iPod shuffle is connected to your computer.

---

iTip: Get Playlists in the Same Order

If you want the songs on your iPod shuffle to be in the exact same order as the ones in the playlist you're choosing to download, go to the Autofill panel at the bottom of the iTunes window and turn off the checkbox for Choose Items Randomly. That way, songs aren't chosen at random, and instead will appear on your iPod shuffle in the same order as your selected playlist in iTunes.

Checking Your Battery While Listening

If you're wondering how much battery charge you have left in your iPod shuffle, you don't have to stop listening to music to find out (like you did in the original version). While you're listening, just quickly turn your iPod shuffle off and then back on, and the battery status LEDs will show you how much charge you have left without stopping the music. Of course, the key here is to be quick about it. Turn it off, then back on, fairly quickly. If the music stops, you're not doing it quickly enough. However, if you're having trouble turning your iPod shuffle off and on quickly enough, perhaps having your music interrupted shouldn't be your biggest concern. (Come on now, seriously, that was pretty funny. It was kind of like a laugh grenade. It goes off about a few seconds after you toss it.)

---

iTip: Finding the Serial Number

Want to know where the serial number for your iPod shuffle is located? If you open the iPod shuffle's clip, you'll see two triangular rows of teeth—one mounted on the unit itself, and one on the clip. The serial number is written on the triangular teeth that are on the body of the unit.

How to Fit More Songs on Your iPod shuffle

If you want to fit as many songs on your iPod shuffle as possible, you can have iTunes automatically convert your MP3, AIFF, and WAV files to AAC (as shown above). Click on your iPod shuffle in the Source list, then click on the Settings tab in the main window, scroll down to Options, and turn on the checkbox for Convert Higher Bit Rate Songs to 128 kbps AAC. Oh yeah, you don't have to worry about altering your original songs—it only converts songs as they're downloaded into your iPod shuffle; the songs in your iTunes Music Library remain untouched.

---

iTip: Getting a Second Dock

Although your iPod shuffle ships with its own Dock, if you decide you need another Dock (one for home, one for the office?), you can order an additional Dock from Apple.com or pick one up at your local neighborhood Apple Store. By the way, having two Docks will give your neighbors Dock envy. It just seems so decadent.

Finding Out How Much Battery Is Left

There's a battery status LED on both the top and bottom of the iPod shuffle (you need it in both places, because since you clip it onto your clothes, there's no telling which end will be up). When you turn on the iPod shuffle, the LEDs give you a quick readout of the battery charge. If the LEDs are green, the battery is pretty well charged. If the lights are amber (yellow), the battery's getting low and before too long you should recharge the battery by putting your iPod shuffle in its Dock and connecting the Dock to your computer's USB port. If the lights are red, you're "runnin' on empty" and soon you will experience "the sounds of silence." If no LED lights come on at all, it's a brick—the battery's dead and you need to recharge before it can do anything—so plug that puppy into your Dock, and the Dock into your computer's USB port for at least two hours, but to get a full charge, leave it plugged in for four.

---

iTip: After You Plug It In

When you plug your iPod shuffle into your Dock, and the Dock into your computer's USB port, the LED status lights (on the top and bottom of your iPod shuffle) will glow yellow, letting you know it's charging. When it's fully charged, it will turn green.

Locking the Buttons

Press-and-hold the Play/Pause button for three seconds

If you're tossing your iPod shuffle into your pocket, you might want to lock the buttons on the front, so your iPod shuffle doesn't accidentally change songs, pause, etc. To do that, just press-and-hold the Play/Pause button for three seconds. The LED status indicators (on the top and bottom) will flash green first, then yellow three times, letting you know that things are safely locked down. If you click on a locked button, yellow LEDs will flash once to let you know that the buttons are locked. To unlock the Control Pad buttons, just hold down the same center Play/Pause button for three more seconds and the LED indicators will flash green three times, letting you know you're unlocked and ready to rock (I know that sounds cheesy—I just couldn't help myself; it just felt so right).

---

iTip: Two Uses for Headphone Jack

The headphone jack on the iPod shuffle does double duty: (1) of course, it's the jack where you plug your headphones in, but it's also (2) where the 1/8–inch plug on your iPod shuffle's Dock plugs into the iPod shuffle itself for charging and syncing to iTunes.

Something Acting Weird? Try Resetting

If something seems to go wrong (your iPod shuffle won't play songs, etc.), you may need to reset your iPod shuffle. Just turn it off by sliding the round On/Off switch on the bottom to the OFF position, and leave it off for 5 seconds. Then turn it back on, and that should do the trick.

---

iTip: Charging Away from Your Computer

If you need to charge your iPod shuffle when you don't have your computer handy (like when you're on vacation), you can plug your iPod shuffle Dock into Apple's optional iPod USB Power Adapter that plugs right into the wall. You can find it at Apple.com or at your local Apple store.

Storing Files on Your iPod shuffle

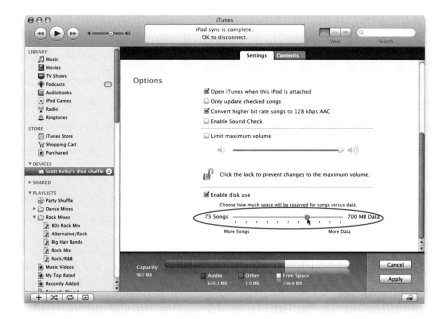

Besides storing music, you can easily configure your iPod shuffle to hold non-audio files, as well, so basically it can double as a flash drive. Here's how: Once your iPod shuffle is connected to your computer, in iTunes click on your iPod shuffle in the Source list, and then click on the Settings tab at the top center of the main window. In the Options section, turn on the checkbox for Enable Disk Use, then move the slider below the checkbox to decide how many songs you want versus how much data you want to be able to store. (As you move the slider, you'll get live feedback showing how much data space versus how many songs you're able to store.) Click Apply and your iPod shuffle will appear on your desktop (on a Mac) or as an available drive on a Windows PC. Now you can just drag-and-drop files right onto it, treating it as though it's a portable flash drive. *Note:* To protect the data on your iPod shuffle, always click on the Eject button in iTunes before you disconnect it (see the next page).

When Do You Need to Eject the iPod shuffle?

If you're just using the iPod shuffle to store songs, you don't need to do anything special when it's time to disconnect your iPod—just pick it up out of the Dock and unplug the USB cable from your computer. Just be sure not to unplug it while it's syncing. An easy way to know if it's safe to unplug is to look up at the status display at the top center of the iTunes window. If iTunes is done syncing your iPod shuffle, the status display will show: "iPod sync is complete. OK to disconnect." However, if you're using your iPod shuffle to store both songs and data (other non-audio files from your computer), you'll first need to ensure that your iPod is done syncing, and then you'll need to click on the Eject button, either in the lower right-hand corner of the iTunes window or to the right of your iPod's name in the Source list. When you do this, iTunes "unmounts" your iPod shuffle, so it's safe to remove your iPod shuffle from your computer without the risk of damaging data. Again, you only have to use the Eject button if you've turned on the Enable Disk Use option in the iPod Shuffle's Settings tab. Otherwise, you can just grab your iPod shuffle and go anytime after you've updated.

How to Restore Your iPod shuffle

Although it's fairly rare, it is possible that one day you'll turn on your iPod shuffle, and if something's gone fairly wrong, after blinking green, your LEDs will then blink amber twice in row, and will repeat this for about 10 seconds. That's the iPod telling you something's gone awry, but it can be easily fixed by restoring the original factory settings. To restore your iPod shuffle, first plug it into the Dock that came with it, then plug that Dock into your computer. When iTunes opens, click on your iPod shuffle in the Source list on the left side of the iTunes window, then click on the Settings tab at the top of the main window. In the Settings, under Version, click on the Restore button. This will erase the contents of your iPod shuffle, reformat the shuffle, restore the original factory settings, and most importantly, fix the problem. Once restored, you can use Autofill to put your songs back onto your iPod shuffle, or you can manually drag-and-drop songs onto it (as detailed earlier in this chapter).

Playing Your Songs in Order

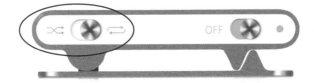

Even though it's the very theme of the iPod shuffle, "Life doesn't have to be random"—because besides playing your songs in a totally random shuffled order, you can also choose to play the songs on your iPod shuffle in the exact order of your playlist, bringing conformity and order to your otherwise chaotic and indiscriminate life (I just put that last part in for dramatic effect. My publisher tells me it sells more books). Anyway, in short, you can play your songs at random or in their playlist order—it's your choice—just use the switch at the bottom left of your iPod shuffle. When the round button's to the left, your iPod shuffle is shuffling your songs in a random order. Slide it to the right, and it's in "Play in Order" mode, which plays the songs in the same order as your playlist. So, in short, free spirits go left, accountants go right.

Unleash Your Inner Control Freak

Want to really exert some serious control over what you thought was a random song player? Then check this out: you can set things up so your highest-rated songs play first, then your four-star songs, and so on. You start by going to iTunes, then click on your iPod shuffle in the Source list on the left side. Then click on the Rating column header to sort your songs from highest rating to lowest rating. Lastly, Control-click (PC: Right-click) on your iPod shuffle in the Source list, and from the contextual menu that appears, choose Copy to Play Order. This updates your iPod shuffle to play your favorite songs first when your Shuffle switch is set to "Play in Order" mode. This is just one example: you could sort by Genre so all your R&B songs play first, or you could sort by Time, so your longest songs play first (do you see where this is going? Total playlist domination). Just don't forget to choose Copy to Play Order after you've sorted your columns so your iPod shuffle gets updated with the same info.

Chapter Fifteen
Cast of Angels
How to Download (and Create Your Own) Podcasts

Podcasting is hot. Burning hot. If you're not familiar with podcasts, they're radio or video shows you can download and listen to (or watch) on your iPod. Now, why are these so hot? 'Cause they're free. Why are they free? 'Cause they're not real. Well, they're usually not real radio or TV shows. They're pretend radio (or fake TV), or neo-radio, which is a much cooler sounding term, but I just coined it, so if you read it elsewhere, you'll know it was I, fake-TV podcaster Kelby, that coined that pithy term. Anyway, podcasting is hot. It is so hot right now that it's like something that is really, really hot. It's got the scorching hot fever of a thousand burning suns. Okay, it's not that hot, but it's hot enough that you'd probably burn your hand, like when you get Mexican food that was cooked in a convection oven and the waiter says, "Be careful, these plates are very hot," but when he sets it down the first thing you do is touch the plate. You can't help it; you've got to see if the waiter was lying. But he's not lying. That plate has the scorching hot fever of a thousand burning suns. In other words, that plate is like a podcast. (This is exactly why my publisher hates it when I drink.) Anyway, this chapter is about the phenomenon of podcasting, which is different than TV shows or movies you buy, because (once again) they're free. Radio podcasts are free too, which is great since your iPod can't receive live FM broadcasts without a special accessory. Speaking of FM, that's where you might hear the title song "Cast of Angels" (get the subtle cast reference?), a totally not bad song by The Marshall McLuhan Project. In fact, that song has the scorching hot fever of...ah, forget it.

Finding Podcasts

Although there are dozens of places to find podcasts, the most convenient is probably right from within the iTunes Store itself. Click on the Podcasts link (on the left side, under iTunes STORE), which will take you directly to the Podcasts area. Apple spotlights some of the newest and most popular podcasts in the center of the page, but I'd like to draw your attention to the left side of the window where you'll find a list of categories, so you can jump right to any area that interests you. For example, if you click on Technology, it gives you the New and Notable podcasts at the top, and a list of 25 of Today's Top Podcasts in Technology on the right side of the window, and the whole center section is devoted to Featured podcasts. These categories are great starting points for uncovering all sorts of cool stuff in the podcasting world.

---

iTip: More Podcasts Elsewhere

The iTunes Store is just one place to search for podcasts. There are loads of podcasting websites (I like podcastalley.com). You'll also find sites that produce their own podcasts, and they'll give you a direct link to subscribe—you just click on it and it takes you directly to that podcast.

Downloading and Subscribing to Podcasts

Okay, let's say you're searching around in the iTunes Store, and you've found a podcast you want to download. Just scroll over to the far right until you see the price field (don't worry, iTunes podcasts are free), and click on the Get Episode button. This downloads just this one episode of that particular podcast. Now, let's say you listen to this one episode, and you love it so much, you don't want to miss a single episode. Then just click on the podcast (within the iTunes Store) and you'll be taken to that podcast's homepage in the iTunes Store. Just to the right of the large graphic, you'll find the only button you need—it says "Subscribe." Click on that button (shown above), and a little dialog will appear asking if that's what you really want to do (basically, it doesn't trust your click-ing ability, and it apparently figures you must have clicked that button by accident). So, since you do in fact want to subscribe (so you get every episode downloaded automati-cally), click the Subscribe button in the dialog, and it downloads the latest edition of that podcast into your iTunes Podcasts Library. This takes you out of the iTunes Store and right to your podcasts, just in case you want to hear that podcast right that minute. So that's it—you can download just one episode of a podcast, or subscribe (still free) to get each new episode automatically as soon as it's updated.

Accessing Your Downloaded Podcasts

Each podcast you've subscribed to appears in your Podcasts playlist, which appears under Library on the left side of the iTunes window. Just click once on Podcasts (shown circled here in red) and your list of downloaded podcasts appears (seen above). To listen to any of these downloaded podcasts, just double-click directly on it (just like you would a song), and if it's an audio podcast, you'll hear it begin (again, just like you would with a song). The date each episode was released is listed in the Release Date column. To check and see if newer episodes have been released, click the Refresh button in the lower right-hand corner of the iTunes window, and iTunes will download the latest episode of that show.

---

iTip: How to Unsubscribe

If you decide you want to stop subscribing to a particular podcast, just click on the podcast, then click on the Unsubscribe button at the bottom-left corner of the Podcasts window.

Watching Video Podcasts

Now, while there are many audio podcasts available, there is also a wide selection of video podcasts. When you subscribe to a video podcast, the show downloads (just like an audio podcast), but when you play the podcast, the video appears in the Artwork box in the bottom-left corner of your iTunes window. How cool is that? To see the video podcast at a larger size, click on the video in that little window, and it then appears in a larger, resizable floating window. You can resize this floating window by clicking-and-dragging the bottom-right corner of the window. I've been doing a weekly video podcast since back in 2005 for Adobe Photoshop users, called *Photoshop®User TV*, and you can find it under the Technology category in the Podcasts section of iTunes. My buddy Matt Kloskowski does two video podcasts: a daily one called *Adobe® Photoshop® CS3 Killer Tips*, and a weekly one called *Adobe® Photoshop® Lightroom Killer Tips*. My friends Corey Barker and RC Concepcion also do a video podcast called *Layers TV*, which covers all Adobe programs. I hope you'll stop by and check them out (yes, that was a plug for our video podcasts, but it was so subtle, I doubt anyone even noticed).

Managing Your Podcasts

So, how often does iTunes check for newly released podcasts? Well, that's up to you. You can have it check daily, weekly, or if you're really strung out on podcasts, you can have it check every hour. You decide how much these podcasts will rule your life by going to the iTunes Preferences (under the iTunes menu on a Mac; the Edit menu on a Windows PC). When the Preferences dialog appears, click on the Podcasts icon and the Podcasts preferences will appear (shown above). This is where you choose how often iTunes should check for new episodes, and when it finds new episodes, whether it should download just the latest episode or all the ones you missed. You can also decide here how many episodes to keep around before they're deleted. Once you make your choices, just click OK, and you've got your podcasts firmly under control. Well, not firmly, but "somewhat" under control.

---

iTip: Sorting Your Podcasts

Once you've downloaded a few podcasts, you can sort your Podcasts Library just like any other iTunes playlist (by dragging-and-dropping them in the order you'd like), except that within a particular podcast, all the individual episodes for that podcast are automatically sorted by Release Date and that order can't be changed.

Downloading Podcasts Not Listed in iTunes

Let's say you run across a website that has a podcast, but they didn't submit their podcast to the iTunes Podcast Directory (so you can't just search for their podcast within the iTunes Store). Well, then, do this: Go under the iTunes Advanced menu and choose Subscribe to Podcast. This brings up a simple (simple meaning plain looking) little dialog (shown above) with a field where you can enter the URL (Web address) of the podcast you want to subscribe to. Enter it, click OK, and it's added to your Podcasts playlist. See, that was easier than you thought it was going to be, wasn't it?

iTip: Enhanced Podcasts

Besides the standard audio and video podcasts, there are also "enhanced" podcasts, which are kind of like DVDs in that they have chapter markers that let you jump to additional tracks, additional graphics, or even live Web links. You access these enhanced features by clicking-and-holding on the Artwork box in the iTunes window, and if the podcast is enhanced, a pop-up menu with other art or chapter markers will appear.

Getting Your Podcasts onto Your iPod

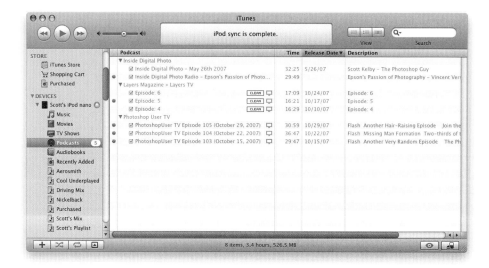

This part is easy—just connect your iPod to your computer and it will automatically update with the latest episode (provided, of course, you left the auto-updating feature turned on. If not, you'll have to choose Sync iPod from the iTunes File menu, but that's so…I dunno…manual).

---

iTip: Choose Which Podcasts Sync

If you don't want all your podcasts transferred to your iPod, you can choose which podcasts get transferred (and which do not) by connecting your iPod to your computer, and clicking on it in the Source list. In the main window, click on the Podcasts tab, turn on the Sync checkbox and click the Selected Podcasts radio button, then turn on the checkboxes beside the podcasts you do want synced on your iPod. Any unchecked podcasts will remain in iTunes, but won't be transferred to your iPod.

Playing Podcasts on Your iPod

It's as easy as playing a song or video. From the main menu, just click on Podcasts and you'll see the names of the various podcasts you've downloaded (not the individual episodes—just the names of the podcasts themselves). Scroll down and click on any podcast to see a listing of the individual episodes on your iPod. To hear (or watch) one of those, scroll down to it then click the Play/Pause button or the center Select button (either one will do the trick).

---

iTip: Finishing a Podcast Later

If you start listening to a podcast within iTunes and then you've got to run, you can plug in your iPod and let it update. When you go back to that podcast on your iPod, it will remember where you were when you paused, and pick up right where you left off. Sweet!

Recording an Audio Podcast (Windows PC)

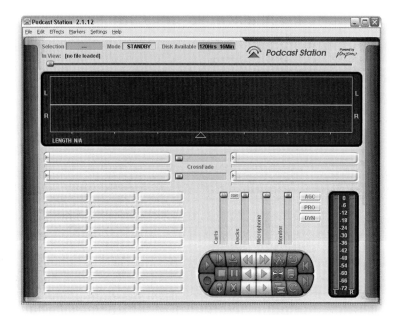

Okay, so you're digging the audio podcast thing, and now you think you might want to try your hand at it. Well, the process is fairly simple, but it starts with buying a USB microphone which plugs into the USB port on your computer. These days there's a wide variety, but you might want to check out the Samson CO1U USB Studio Condenser Mic, which works well for podcasting, and works with both Macs and PCs (I found it new on Amazon.com for less than $90). If you prefer to use a headset USB mic, take a look at the Andrea NC-7100 USB headset mic (it's around $79.95), or the Plantronics .Audio 510 USB Headset (which you can buy right from Apple's online store for around $69.95). Once you've got your USB mic, you'll need some software to record your podcast. If you've got a Mac, you probably already have Apple's GarageBand (it comes preinstalled on Macs), and it has a whole audio-recording/podcasting thing built right in (more on this later), but if you're using a Windows PC, then check out the award-winning Podcast Station, which not only records your audio (complete with a built-in software audio mixer and editor), but also includes tools to help you actually publish your finished podcast, as well. It's only $59.95, but they have a 30-day free trial version you can download from their website at www.podcaststation.com so you can try before you buy.

Recording an Audio Podcast (Mac)

If you bought a Macintosh computer within the past few years, you've already got GarageBand (a brilliant software recording studio and much more) preinstalled on your Mac—just look in your Applications folder and you'll find it there. If, for some reason, you don't have it, it's part of Apple's iLife '08 software suite, which you can buy from Apple's online store for $79 (but my guess is—you already have some version of GarageBand on your Mac, so look in your Applications folder first. You'll need version 3 or higher). GarageBand lets you easily (and I mean easily) record and edit your audio podcast (with built-in studio effects), and it also lets you add cover artwork, create chapter markers (so people can jump directly to different parts of your podcast), embed live Web links so people listening to your podcast in iTunes can click and jump to sites you mention during your show, it comes with royalty-free background music tracks, and it even lets you add and edit tags about your podcast (the author's name, the title, and a description of your podcast) so people can find your podcast in Apple's iTunes podcast directory. Not only that, it actually builds a webpage for your podcast for you, where people can listen on this new webpage, or subscribe to your podcast on iTunes. That ain't bad for free software that comes with your Mac, eh? I highly recommend going to Apple's website and watching their free tutorial on how to get going with GarageBand and podcasting (it's amazingly simple once you watch their tutorial). It's found at www.apple.com/ilife/tutorials/#garageband-podcast-51.

Creating a Video Podcast (Windows PC)

If you've created a video movie you want to publish as a podcast, you have to com-
press and format the movie so it plays on the iPod. One way to do that is by using
Apple's QuickTime Pro for Windows for $29.99 from the Apple online Store (go to
Apple.com, then click on the Store tab up top). In fact, QuickTime Pro will even let you
record audio podcasts right from within QuickTime Pro itself. Anyway, what you really
need QuickTime Pro for is to convert your video movie to the iPod size and format. You
do that by launching QuickTime Pro, then going under QuickTime Pro's File menu and
choosing Open, then opening your video movie. Once your movie is open in Quick-
Time Pro, go under the File menu again, but this time choose Export. When the Export
dialog appears, choose Movie to iPod (320x240) from the pop-up menu. It may take
a few minutes to convert the movie, but when it's done, you're ready to move on to
posting your podcast on a website that includes an RSS feed.

Creating a Video Podcast (Mac)

Besides creating super-quick and easy audio podcasts, Apple's GarageBand (which comes free with your Mac—just look in your Applications folder) also does a great job with video podcasting (take a moment, go back a few pages, and read the entry called "Recording an Audio Podcast [Mac]" to acquaint yourself with GarageBand. Plus, there's a link to a video tutorial you'll want there, as well). The big difference with creating a video podcast in GarageBand is that you'll take the video footage you've already created (maybe you edited it together using Apple's free iMovie video software, or perhaps it's video from your DV camera that you want to narrate over) and, using the Media Browser in GarageBand, you just add that movie into your podcast. Once it's there, you can add background music, a voice-over narration track, cover art, chapter markers, the info you need for Apple's iTunes podcast directory, and it will publish all of this on a webpage for you automatically.

Going "On the Air" (Step One)

All right, now you're almost ready to go live with your podcast. I say *almost* because there are three steps you have to do before it finally "goes live." It takes a few minutes (the first time you set it up), but once you've set this all up, subsequent podcasts are much quicker. Here (in short) are the three steps, and on this page, we'll cover the first:

(1) The first step is to upload the audio or video file to the Web. You have to do this because you have to have a URL (Web address) where your podcast is located on the Web. You can upload it to your own website, a friend's website, or you can upload it to one of the free services (like Ourmedia.org [shown above], which will happily host your podcast for free. Like their service, registration is also free, so don't let the "I don't have a website" thing hold you back). Once you've uploaded your podcast to the Web, write down the exact URL (Web address) where your podcast is located on the Web. You'll need this address in the next step.

---

iTip: Finding Your Podcast

By the way, to quickly find that compressed podcast on your hard disk, just Control-click (PC: Right-click) on the podcast in your iTunes Music Library and choose Show in Finder or Show in Windows Explorer from the pop-up menu that appears. The folder your podcast currently resides in will then appear front and center.

The Second Step: Creating a Blog

(2) You do Step Two once your audio or video file is uploaded to a website (your own, a friend's, or a hosting service like Ourmedia.org, etc.) and you know the exact URL (Web address) of your uploaded file. Now, you need to post that URL on a webpage that supports RSS feeds, like Blogger.com. In fact, I'm going to recommend that you head over to Blogger.com (shown above), sign up for a free blog of your own (it's super easy), and post your link there. Now, some advanced podcasters might recommend other methods (like Movable Type or WordPress), but we're not advanced podcasters (yet). We're just starting out, and Blogger.com is free, it couldn't be user-friendlier (a gerbil could create its own blog on Blogger.com), and best of all, it does the job you need at this point. So, one day you might outgrow Blogger.com, but for basic podcasting, it works wonderfully well. So, go to Blogger.com, and create your free blog (it takes three steps, which in total take about two minutes). In your first post, you'll want to write a brief description of your blog. Then, on a separate line below the description, type in the following: <a href="(insert the exact URL [Web address] where you uploaded your audio podcast file)"> </a>. Click the Publish Post button, and you've done it—you have a blog.

A Little More of the Second Step

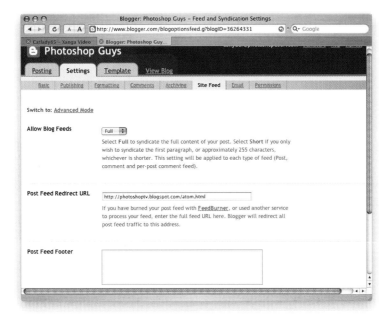

Once you've got your blog up and running, you'll now log in to the Dashboard area (where you can add new blog posts, or edit your existing posts). Near the top of this page, click on the Settings link and you'll see a row of links across the top of your page. Click on the one named Site Feed and next to Post Feed Redirect URL you'll see a new URL (shown above). That's the one you need to copy exactly for the final step. So copy that, will ya?

Submit Your Podcast to the iTunes Directory

(3) The third and final step is to submit your podcast website URL (the one you copied in the previous step) to Apple's iTunes podcast directory. To get there, click on the Podcasts link at the top left of the iTunes Store homepage. Scroll down to the bottom of the Podcasts page and click on the Submit a Podcast link on the left. Then just paste (or type) in your exact URL, click the Continue button, follow the simple steps, and sit back and wait to hear from Apple that you've been accepted (and unless you had some really super naughty stuff in your podcast, or you just totally messed everything up, you'll be in the directory in no time). All that is the easy part. Getting the word out about your podcast, creating some buzz, and building an audience that wants to download and watch each episode of your show—that's the really hard part, and thankfully for me, it's beyond the scope of this book (but Amazon.com and BarnesandNoble.com both carry books on how to market your podcast, so make sure you give a look there).

Appendix

Recommended Dose

A Peek at My Own Personal, Ultra-Secret, Yet Surprisingly Way-Cool Playlists

▶▶ Okay, this last part isn't really a chapter. It's too short to be a chapter, and it really doesn't tell you how to use your iPod. So what is it? Some ideas to help you build your musical collection. And to that end I'm going to pull aside the veil of secrecy, remove the cone of silence, and openly share some of my very own playlists, thereby stripping away any pretense and baring my musical soul to you, my esteemed reader (and contributor to my children's college fund). Basically, what I did was gather some of my playlists and publish them as iMixes on the iTunes Store (samples follow, and the iTunes Store links to them appear on each page). If you want to hear a 30-second preview of any of my recommended songs, you can do that right from my iMixes, and if you like one of those songs, you can buy it right there, too. Now, I don't get any kickbacks or royalties from Apple—but if you download one (or all) of these songs (yes, just one click and you can buy the entire playlist), there will be a time when you and I are both playing the exact same song at the exact same time—and from that moment on there will be a connection, a sacred bond between us that can never be broken. Oh yeah, I asked this book's original tech editor, Terry White, to share one of his playlists, too; but if you buy his songs, there's no bond. Sorry, that's just the way he is. By the way, the chapter title came from a song by Rico, from his album *Violent Silences*. If I had made that album, I would've named it "Abbey Road."

Scott's Big Hair Rock Mix Playlist

A mix of my favorite 1980s and early '90s commercial rock songs

I published these songs as an iMix on the iTunes Store. You can find this list (and buy the songs online) at **http://phobos.apple.com/WebObjects/MZStore.woa/wa/viewPublishedPlaylist?id=52478**.

Scott's '80s Club Dance Mix Playlist

What we danced to in the clubs back then, in our sport coats with the sleeves rolled

I published these songs as an iMix on the iTunes Store. You can find this list (and buy the songs online) at **http://phobos.apple.com/WebObjects/MZStore.woa/ wa/viewPublishedPlaylist?id=166339**.

Scott's Old School Funk Mix

Songs to make you smile when you're already in a really good mood

I published these songs as an iMix on the iTunes Store. You can find this list (and buy the songs online) at **http://phobos.apple.com/WebObjects/MZStore.woa/wa/ viewIMix?id=202595568.**

Jordan's Radio Disney-Like Playlist

The songs my 11-year-old son likes on AM Radio Disney

I published these songs as an iMix on the iTunes Store. You can find this list (and buy the songs online) at **http://phobos.apple.com/WebObjects/MZStore.woa/wa/viewIMix?id=267985767**.

Terry's Top 25

My Tech Editor Terry White's top 25 favorite songs—Terry's a freak

Terry published these songs as an iMix on the iTunes Store. You can find this list (and buy the songs online) at **http://phobos.apple.com/WebObjects/MZStore.woa/wa/viewPublishedPlaylist?id=165878.**

Index

A

AAC format, 52, 193
About screen, 53
AC power adapter, 294
accessories, 289–304
  armbands, 300
  car-related, 83–93
  colorized iPods, 299
  Crystal Film Cover, 296
  FM radio tuner, 295
  headphones, 301–303
  Incase Neoprene Sleeve, 297
  Nike + iPod Sports Kit, 298
  remote control, 110
  speaker systems, 37, 290–292
  Universal Dock, 293
  USB Power Adapter, 294
  wireless network device, 304
Account Info page, 223
Address Book, 75, 165
Adobe Photoshop Album, 122, 124, 167
Adobe Photoshop Elements, 122, 124, 166, 167
AirPort Express, 304
AirTunes, 304
alarm function, 61, 151
album art
  browsing, 44, 147, 286
  Cover Flow view, 44, 147, 286
  deleting, 268
  downloading, 217, 232
  getting for CD covers, 232
  Grouped Artwork View, 285
  iTunes display options, 267, 285
  substitutes for, 140
albums
  completing, 214
  gapless playback of, 200
  On-The-Go playlists and, 56
  printing lists of, 270
  rating, 252
  seeing songs on, 143
  shuffle feature for, 145, 272
  Smart Playlists of, 259
  See also **photo albums**
Allowance feature, 224
Apple.com, 3, 14

Apple logo, 278
Apple Store
  battery replacement, 36
  ITS gift certificates, 224
Apple TV, 117
AppleCare plan, 36
armbands, 300
artists
  finding songs by, 212
  ITS Alert feature, 213, 215
  playlists based on, 145
Audible.com, 65
audio
  file formats, 193
  streaming, 227, 228
audio CDs. *See* **CDs**
audio podcasts
  listening to, 328, 333
  recording, 334–335
  See also **podcasts**
audiobooks, 65, 149, 312
authorizing computers, 226, 229
Auto Kit for iPod, 86
auto-complete feature, 152
Autofill feature, 308, 309, 310
auto-import feature, 191
auto-launch option, 129
automotive accessories. *See* **car-related accessories**
auto-naming feature, 192
auto-updating, 72
auxiliary input plug, 85
AV Cable connection, 110, 131

B

backing up
  songs, 218, 265
  videos, 113
Backlight
  battery life and, 29, 31
  turning on, 30
Backlight Timer, 31
Barker, Corey, 329
battery
  charging, 33–34, 294
  replacing, 36
  slow drain of, 35
battery life
  Backlight and, 29, 31
  Brightness slider and, 115

W

X

Y

Z

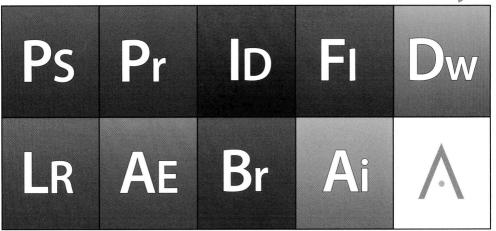